THINGS THEY NEVER TELL YOU BEFORE YOU SAY "YES"
The Nonmusical Tasks of the Church Musician

Robin Knowles Wallace

Abingdon Press
Nashville

THINGS THEY NEVER TELL YOU BEFORE YOU SAY "YES"
The Nonmusical Tasks of the Church Musician

Copyright © 1994 by Abingdon Press

All rights reserved.

This book is printed on acid-free, recycled paper.

Library of Congress Cataloging-in-Publication Data

Wallace, Robin Knowles.
    Things they never tell you before you say "yes" : the nonmusical tasks of the church musician / Robin Knowles Wallace.
    p. ; cm.
    ISBN 0-687-28165-2
    1. Church musicians—Employment.   2. Church musicians—Job descriptions.
I. Title.
ML3795.W28   1994
264'.2—dc20
                                        94-11010
                                          CIP
                                          MN

97 98 99 00 01 02 03 — 10 9 8 7 6 5 4 3 2

MANUFACTURED IN THE UNITED STATES OF AMERICA

/

To John, Laura, and Grace-Anne,
and all the singers of the Song

Contents

Cast of Characters

Hope Church

Jill, adult choir director
Lillian, choir librarian
Sam, adult robe handler
Susan, Marvin, parents of
  children
Mary, child's parent and
  worship committee
  member
Harry, child's parent and
  finance chairperson
Sharon, organist
Rev. John
Millard, worship
  chairperson
Grace, children's choir
  director
David and Mike, worship
  committee members
June and Millie, adult choir
  members
Yvonne, children's choir
  helper

Pat, Ad Council chair
Harry, finance chair
Roy, Ad Council member,
  Staff-Parish Committee

Second Church

Gil, director of music
Pastor Lee (she)
Sue, worship chair
Laura, substitute organist
Jim, Karen, bell choir
  members
Carol, bell choir member and
  children's choir volunteer
Sally, finance chairperson

Others

Tom, workshop leader
Gloria, experienced musician
  in town

Introduction

"Now you've done it," or "Welcome to the wonderful world of church music!"

You have agreed to direct a choir at church. You know how to conduct in 4/4, 3/4, and even 6/8, but what about planning for rehearsals, managing the choir room, conducting smooth relationships with other staff, choir, and congregation?

You love to play the piano, and your church's organist just left for a "better" job. You've been asked to play—now, where is the key for the locked piano?

Someone has donated enough money for your church to purchase a full three-octave set of handbells and the person who negotiated the deal was just moved out of state by his company. You are now in charge of the handbells and starting a handbell choir. Where do you find help?

Church music is a wonderful way to combine two of the most important things to people like you and me—faith in God and love of God's gift of music. The details involved in running an effective church music program can enable faith and music to happen or they can drown us in the process itself. This book is written to help you navigate the waters, to throw you some lifelines. You are not alone; the Bible has promised this. Claim it for yourself and for your church music program.

Here you will find stories of how people at two different churches tackle the joys and challenges of church music leadership. The stories have been adapted from real situations, and the names have been changed. They are presented here to remind you that you are not alone. Others have walked these paths before you, and others are around you now who can help and encourage you.

Perhaps a brief word about my own story can serve as an introduction to what is to follow. I was asked to play for church when I began high school, after the sudden departure of the church organist. I had one month of organ lessons (to add to my years of piano lessons) before beginning to play for worship. I had sung in children's choirs and had been fascinated by worship all my life. But playing for church was a whole new world. Some of my favorite times stem from practicing in that beautiful sanctuary (on a not-so-beautiful organ!) after school, learning the hymns of the church.

I continued to play for church during college, and began directing when the choir director moved. I was studying music in school, and thought that being a church musician was as close as I could get to heaven! God and music, expressing faith through music, making heavenly sounds together, teaching children the history of the church through hymns, reawakening the Spirit in adults through prayerful singing—what a life! (I was young and naive, and didn't worry about things like making a living in those days!)

Early on, I was very fortunate in two ways. The first pastor I worked with, who happened to be my father, was interested in and knowledgeable about worship and was a good long-range planner. During my college days I made the acquaintance of an ordained minister of music at a nearby church. He introduced me to the organizations that supplied me with journals and new ideas monthly and with wonderful convocations to attend, where I met church musicians from all over the country. This support and the affirmation that I was on the right track in working with not just music, but the Spirit too, was invaluable.

I did go on to get advanced degrees in church music and theology, but my commitment to the local church remains constant. No matter where you are, God is there and music can help you feel the Spirit. One of the most delightful choirs I had was the smallest, only ten singers, but oh, the sounds they could make, and the fellowship we had!

So now I've worked in churches in several different states for over twenty-five years—large churches, small churches, with tiny children and great-grandparents, with singers and ringers—both playing and directing. I've grown through my experiences and I think I've helped my choirs to grow, musically and spiritually.

I've learned a lot from other musicians, from pastors, from choir members, and from people in the congregation. I hope you will find here a new idea or new perspective that will help you in your work.

To God be the glory!

Chapter One:
Managing the Choir Room

"What is that mountain of music on my desk, and why do the choir robes smell?"

O h, no!" Jill's spirits sank as she opened the choir room door. Just last week she had responded to the enthusiasm of the staff-parish committee and agreed to direct the adult choir. Jill had substituted for the director several times last year and enjoyed leading the choir in worship.

But Jill was not prepared for what greeted her in the choir room, which wore signs of midsummer neglect. The director's desk was piled foot-high with journals, catalogues, packets of music, and unopened mail. "I'd better tackle that mess when I've got a whole day to spend," thought Jill.

"Maybe I'll start with the music files and pick some pieces to start with in September." But to Jill's dismay, the files resembled the desk. Two drawers of the cabinet were too full to close, assorted pieces of music lay on top of the cabinet and were strewed across a nearby table.

Discouraged, Jill's mind jumped ahead to Christmas. "Maybe I should decide on a cantata first and then work from there." She opened the robe closet, where the cantatas were shelved above. An unpleasant odor greeted her, with the realization that the choir had blithely hung up their robes at the end of a hot, humid June and the robes had been closed up for six weeks.

Jill slumped down on the piano bench. She had pictured herself enthusiastically leading rehearsals and proudly conducting anthems in worship. Nothing had prepared her for these mundane "house-keeping" tasks. Disheartened, she spread her fingers out to play a full chord on the piano. But no comfort was to be found—even the piano was out of tune!

Welcome to the real world of church music—it's not always glamorous! Yet just as God made order out of chaos in creation, so also part of your task as church musician is to create order in the choir room and then in the music program.

When Jill left the choir room after her brief discouraging tour, she spent the car ride home in prayer for guidance and strength. On arriving home she found her church directory and called two friends from the choir. Lillian had been the choir librarian before their last director had decided he would do it all. Sam had retired from work last year and always seemed willing to help. Supported by her friends, Jill entered the choir room the next evening ready to tackle the mess.

The Desk

Like any other task, once systems are in order maintenance can run smoothly. Still, even the most organized among us get backed up at times and need to reorganize.

Let's begin with the worst first, by reducing that mountain of music and mail on the desk to create a space to work and plan.

Journals

Jill has four piles to start with: church music journals, music catalogues, new music, and miscellaneous mail. It is helpful to have shelves or magazine boxes for the journals. These can be handy if the choir room has plenty of room for storing journals. If not, consider putting back issues in an area of the church library, keeping only the current year's issues in the choir room. Either way, separate journals by title, then order by date—oldest to most recent.

Catalogues

You will receive many catalogues that you will never use. There is nothing sacred about saving catalogues. If your church just bought new choir robes last year, don't keep any robe catalogues or fliers. Things will change before you're ready to buy again and most often the catalogues will track you down by the time you need them. Do the same with catalogues of instruments, risers, and folders, as these are not frequently purchased items.

If you see a catalogue you just love the look of but don't foresee using in the next year or two, tear off the cover or inside page with their address and phone, file the page in your catalogue file, and toss (or recycle) the rest. For the catalogues that you will refer to often, keep only the current issue because prices constantly change. Catalogues might be kept in a magazine box, file drawer, or on a shelf.

New Music

Review packets of music can represent a major headache for musicians. It can take forever to play through all the music that arrives on our desks unsolicited yet we don't want to chance missing a single great piece. Jill may plan today to get this music into reasonable stacks, perhaps by season or voicing. Then she can parcel out the task of going through it at her own speed. When she is ready, there are several screening procedures to choose from in dealing with new music.

1. The tapes that many publishers include with the music can be listened to in the car or even while doing dishes. Do bear in mind that most often these are professional singers and your choir has its own strengths and weaknesses. Don't be seduced by the music; be sure to check the texts carefully.
2. Over time, we often settle into using only one particular publisher. While this may make our choices more manageable it can severely limit our choir's repertoire. Each choir's repertoire should include varieties of anthems to appeal to and stretch our congregation's understanding of praise.
3. To avoid the subjectivity of publishers, we may choose to belong to a music review club. While this will introduce us to a wider variety of publishers, bear in mind that even review clubs can have a bias toward certain types of music.
4. Reading sessions at workshops or day-long sessions with composers or a particular publishing house can be an enjoyable way to read through new anthems. While you're singing, if a particular

anthem strikes you, try to imagine your choir singing it, not the multitude of glorious voices around you. In addition to the repertoire reading at these sessions be sure to make or renew musical acquaintances. Some of the best ideas at these sessions often come out over informal luncheon discussions.

5. Sitting alone at the piano, though incapable of providing the choral sound, can be fruitful. It can be scheduled whenever you need a creative, reflective time to focus your energy on new music.

Whatever method you choose, keep the following criteria in mind. Skim the text: Is it sound theology? Is the poetry particularly beautiful or moving? Does it lift up the praise and concerns of your congregation? Does it "ring true" to Christian experience? Listen to the music: Does it match the text in mood and meter? Is it singable? Does it have a "fresh" sound, or is it particularly beautiful or moving? Are the parts within the vocal range of your choir? Does the accompaniment complement the vocal parts and is it sufficient to support your particular choir?

Each anthem goes into one of three piles. YES!—the few exceptional anthems that give you goose bumps. MAYBE—good solid anthems, perhaps particularly appropriate for a special occasion, or a "goal" anthem that would help teach a particular skill. NO—poor theology, boring music, trite in any way, inappropriate for your choir or congregation.

Ideally YES! will be your smallest pile (you can't do everything new next year, the choir and the budget won't stand it) and NO will be the largest pile—ready to toss in the garbage. Please don't clutter your choir room or workspace with anthems you can't bear to admit are not well written. Just because it's published doesn't mean it's good.

Use these same three piles with music from reading sessions, music review clubs, publisher's packets, and tapes. If the tapes do not come with anthem copies mark Y, M, N on the listing that came with the tape.

Leave the YES! pile on top of the piano or on your desk to use in your next music planning session. Put the MAYBE pile in a folder near at hand to review at your next planning session. (You threw the NOs away, didn't you?)

The Mail

Now the desk is beginning to look a bit less threatening. Journals have been moved to shelves, magazine boxes, or files. Catalogues have been sorted and filed. A plan is set to bring that mountain of music down into two manageable piles (YES! and MAYBE). There's still some mail for Jill to deal with, about a dozen pieces. Let's help her deal with each of these representative samples.

- A "thank you" from the host choir for this choir's participation in an ecumenical festival. Jill makes a note to share it at the next choir rehearsal and also makes notes on her calendar and a note for the church secretary's calendar about the next festival's time and place. Then the note can be posted on a choir bulletin board, placed in a scrapbook, or tossed.
- A bill from the organ technician, who came before Easter to tune the organ. Put in "to do" file. (See chapter 4.) Mark ASAP on it!
- A list from the administrative council listing all important dates for the coming year. Put in "to do" file. (See chapter 2).
- Renewal notices for two church journals. When Jill was filing the journals she found one to be very readable while the others seemed better suited to their former director with its technical discussions. Jill decides to cancel the technical journal for this year and renew the one that looked more helpful. Since there are old issues of the technical journal in the choir files Jill knows she can decide another year to subscribe to it if she feels it will be helpful. Before submitting the renewal to the church treasurer Jill notes the cost of the subscription on the list of music expenses kept handy in the desk.
- Two advertising fliers. Both are for items Jill doesn't need, so she tosses them.
- An invitation to a workshop in the fall. Jill figures she needs all the help she can get and the cost seems reasonable. She decides to check the continuing education budget to be sure it can cover the costs and then she will register.
- An invitation from the denomination's women's group president for the choir to provide music at the district annual meeting. Put in "to do" file. (See chapter 5.)
- Three notices of concerts in the community. Jill tosses the two that have already passed and posts the third, upcoming, on the choir bulletin board.

Supplies

Now that the desk top is manageable, Jill checks that the desk and room include everything she needs to work.
1. Church stationery, paper, envelopes, and stamps
2. Pens that work
3. Pencils (enough for each choir member plus extras)
4. Pencil sharpener that works
5. File folders for desk and music library (if needed)
6. Chalk and erasers for chalkboard
7. Music manuscript paper (for transposing parts for instruments, composing descants or responses, or for the organist)
8. Tape, for mending music
9. Denominational calendar listing church seasons and special Sundays
10. Local church calendar, in view at all times
11. Thumbtacks for bulletin board
12. Scratch paper for notes
13. Postcards for absentees
14. Birthday cards
15. Plain typing paper or legal pads for planning, robe lists, and schedules for choir members

While Jill waits for Lillian (who is busy with the choral library) to reach a stopping place, she checks out the choir bulletin board. The fancy border is very faded. New borders, either musical or seasonal, can be found at a local teacher's supply store. The bulletin board also contains notices of concerts now long past. Jill takes these down and either tosses them or tears them into four sheets for scrap paper if one side is blank (good stewardship!).

Jill notes that some pictures of past choir programs have been on the board a long time and are getting bent. It is time to either frame them or file them in a choir scrapbook.

Tomorrow, with her list of needed items, Jill will stop by the church office to see if these supplies are on hand. She will find out if they are regularly bought by the office staff, or if she needs to buy them, either by putting them on the church account at a particular store or by submitting a voucher for reimbursement.

The Choir Library

Meanwhile Lillian has been tackling the choir library. Since the stack of mixed-up music is large, Lillian asks some elementary-aged children to help separate the anthems, using the covers as guides. Lillian provides an ice cream cone reward, makes some friends, gets the anthems separated, and is free to straighten the music files while the children tackle the other tasks.

Each piece of music gets its own folder or music box. Folders are less expensive but wear out faster and require file drawers. While music boxes are more expensive up front they last longer and require only shelves for storage.

There are two basic filing systems: (1) alphabetical by title or composer's last name, and (2) numerical. Alphabetical filing has the advantage of making it possible to go directly to the file and find the piece you're looking for, provided all are agreed on whether titles are filed under "A," "The," or first important word and whether composers or arrangers are used as file names. If you use this system, follow the hymnal alphabetizing scheme: first word in title, composers by recognized spelling (Tchaikovsky, not Tzaikovsky). The disadvantage to this system is that each time you buy a new piece, everything in the file drawers after that piece will need to be moved back. To a certain extent this problem can be avoided by only filling each drawer three-quarters full, but eventually it will return.

Numerical filing has the advantage of filling the drawers in sequence. Each piece of music is given a number, usually hand-written in the upper right-hand corner of the piece. The number is noted on the file cards for the piece. Each new piece takes the next number and goes behind the last filed piece. The disadvantage to this system is not being able to go directly to the files—you must search the card or computer file for the number first.

It is helpful to note on each file folder or box the title, composer, voicing, and number of copies of each piece. Many books suggest that each piece also have a choir member's folder number. This does make for super organization and will let you know who still has that particular piece in their folder or at home. But our choir librarian has never used this system, finding that music doesn't disappear that often and that numbering all the pieces, matching up folders, and sequencing each as it is returned just isn't worth the effort.

While the children sort the unfiled music, Lillian works on the filed music, checking that files are in order, that each file is what it says it is, counting quickly the number of copies in each file and writing it on the folder. Ordinarily this counting would be done each time the music is handed in, but things got a bit sloppy during the last director's tenure (while he tried to do it all himself).

The counting of copies is an important part of enabling various pieces to be used. It is not legal to buy twenty copies of an anthem and then photocopy five extra copies when the choir grows. When the choir grows (Hallelujah!) or when copies get lost, new music needs to be purchased. One way to do this would be to keep a constant number of copies of each piece in the files at all times. However, if your choir library is like most it will include a number of pieces that are old or overused and will not be used in the near future. Some pieces may lend themselves to use by a small ensemble as opposed to the entire choir so fewer copies will be needed.

By planning in large blocks (see chapter 2) you will have sufficient time to check the number of copies for each anthem and order enough to have copies for each member of the choir (and the director and accompanist). Having a sufficient number of copies of music saves scrounging for enough copies in rehearsal, depending on who is here this week and who had music last week.

While we are on the subject of sufficient copies, please also remember that soloists will need two legal copies, one for themselves and one for their accompanist. It is not good stewardship to copy music; it is illegal and unethical. DON'T DO IT! As a Christian and a church worker (paid or volunteer) you are a model for behavior. Keep everything above board. Purchase your copies and do not let your church secretary or choir members copy illegally for you or the music program.

Lillian may decide also to keep a director's file and an accompanist's file. They would include one copy of each anthem in the choir files, often with the director's conducting marking or the accompanist's organ registrations. Directors often like to play through music they are considering using and it can be a headache for the choir librarian to have to refile single copies of fifty anthems. So Lillian checks that the director's and accompanist's files are in order, containing one copy of each anthem in the files for each folder, in the order that the rest of the files are in. These folders go in a special place in the choir room, generally near the director's desk or the piano.

Another day Lillian will coordinate the file folders and the card file, with help from Jill and/or other friends. Lillian hopes that someday the library will be on computer. But for now she has three sets of cards:

Season
- Advent
- Christmas
- New Year's
- Epiphany
- Transfiguration
- Lent
- Palm Sunday
- Maundy Thursday
- Good Friday
- Easter
- Ascension
- Pentecost
- Christian education
- Communion
- Thanksgiving
- All Saints' Day
- General
- Instruments

Composer
- Title name
- Arranger
- Voicing
- Publisher and number
- Number of copies

Title
- Composer/ arranger
- Voicing
- Publisher and number
- Number of copies
- Date performed

The composer and title cards will be alphabetically filed. For ease of planning it is helpful to have the seasonal cards grouped by season/subject. If you use anthems with extra instruments frequently, it may help to group those by flute, violin, trumpet, bells, and so on.

It will help Lillian if she can pull the anthem folder and call out its information while different persons check each card entry (composer, title, season, instruments).

Robes

Sam had perhaps the easiest job for now, though not necessarily the most pleasant. Before the new choir year begins the ill-smelling choir robes need to be cleaned and mended. Sam first checks that the bottom of zippers are secure and that hooks and eyes and hems are not in need of mending. If there is a lot of mending to be done Sam will call June, who loves to sew and has assisted in making costumes for choir programs.

Then Sam calls two or three dry cleaners in the area and asks about their bulk rates and/or church discount. Pick-up, pressing, delivery, and billing round out Sam's questions. This year there is enough money in the budget for bulk rate, pressing, and delivery. Next year Sam may suggest that money be saved by having each member clean their own robe after Christmas and in June. Sam is willing to check that each person does this.

Sam bundles up the robes and takes them to the dry cleaners. There he is assured that the robes will be delivered back to the church during building hours and that a bill will be sent to the church to the attention of the music department. Sam then arranges to have the church secretary or custodian open the choir room for the delivery.

When the robes are returned Sam puts them in numerical order, with the numbers of the robes matching the number on the hanger, and he finds the robes that have fitted sleeves for the director and accompanists. He will have to ask Jill if she wants the robe with fitted sleeves for directing or if she feels more comfortable in her old robe. Then he checks the old robe listing. Some updating will need to wait until choir reassembles in the fall since the list contains some cross-outs and some double-listing of names.

Sam volunteers to update the list at the end of the first rehearsal. He recalls that last year the robe lengths were not uniform on the singers and he volunteers to help check this as well. He remembers that when he first joined the choir, the ease with which a robe was found for him felt welcoming. Sam posts the tentative list in the robe closet. In some choirs robe numbers match folder numbers, but since Lillian prefers not to number folders that step is omitted here.

Choir Folders

Lillian will retain the previous system of having the choir folders in cubbies alphabetically arranged. She begins with the persons who sang last year and includes four extra folders for potential new members.

When Jill has selected music for the fall, Lillian will spend time assembling copies for each folder, doing it herself if given sufficient lead time. The alternative is to have copies available as members come into rehearsal, but this causes problems with absentees and latecomers. Lillian and Jill agree that using rehearsal time passing out music feels wasteful, so Jill agrees to always let Lillian know about new music at least by the Sunday before the rehearsal in which it is needed.

Lillian uses summertime to go through and clean out old music, tissues, and bulletins, checking that folders are in shape, and that hymnals and sharpened pencils are also in the cubbies.

When new music arrives in the mail, Jill will first check that it is what she ordered. Then Lillian stamps it with a church stamp (a return address stamp from an office supply store) and numbers it if she is using a numerical filing system. She puts a new label for the music on a box or folder, enters it on the card or computer file, puts copies in the director's and accompanist's files, and files the folder or box.

New Robes

When rehanging the cleaned adult choir robes, Sam takes a peek at the children's choir robes. They are in especially bad shape—hems falling, zippers not working, and material fading in spots. When Jill takes Sam and Lillian out to lunch to thank them for their help, Sam asks if perhaps it is time to get new children's robes. Jill suggests to Grace, her children's choir director, that the question about robes be taken to her children's choir parents' meeting later that month.

The choir parents agree wholeheartedly to replace the robes. Suggestions fly: Mary has seen a pattern in the back of a pattern catalogue and is willing to help sew, Harry would like the robes to match the adult choir, Susan is willing to head a spaghetti dinner to raise funds, Marvin knows several people who might be willing to donate money. Grace designates a "robe committee." The first agenda item of the committee is to check with the pastor and finance chairperson about adding this fund-raising project to the church's schedule. Jill sits down and writes guidelines for Grace's committee based on her memories of buying the adult robes three years ago:

1. Contact several companies for styles, prices, time between ordering and receiving, fabric swatches and color samples, method of cleaning, amount of down payment, and time to pay off balance.
2. If allowed to raise funds from congregation, publicize widely for at least a month in bulletin, newsletters, among various groups in the church, and on bulletin boards. Many persons are very willing to support the music program, especially for visible things like robes.
3. In choosing color, consider sanctuary colors and their permanence or impermanence (if the church is getting new sanctuary carpet in the near future, pick robes after that or work with whomever is picking the carpet colors), hymnal color, color of other choir's robes. Visual harmony in the sanctuary is as important as musical harmony.
4. Order robes for future needs—new members will come in and children will grow. Have a variety of sizes.
5. Measure for uniform length. Children can be especially sensitive about robes too short or too long. Plan for steps or risers, so that people won't be tripping over their robes going up or down.
6. With children, consider ease of putting on and taking off their robes. If they can do it without assistance, it will be a big help on Sunday morning.

7. For uniformity, purchasing robes is easiest. You may be able to save money and get folks working together if robes are sewn by members of the congregation, but it is a difficult project to pull off. If you have a group of seamstresses who have been making costumes for years, it might work. Children's robes, because they are often worn less frequently might be easiest for this group to do.

8. Be ready for "color" battles as persons stake out their choice. The easiest and most liturgical choice will be a neutral color that can be varied by stoles in liturgical colors. Avoid faddish colors because these robes will be used for years.

9. Be patient. The robes are going to be used for many years by the choir, so be willing to spend a little time and make a good choice.

10. If members of the congregation are concerned about the cost, be ready to explain why robes are important to the choir and to the church.

    - Robes subdue the personal element and equalize choir members. This avoids a fashion show or competition in the choir loft.
    - Robes provide an appearance of unity, a sense of the common purpose of the choir.
    - Robes give focus to the visual element of the choir.

Jill includes on the list one of her own convictions about robes. Directors and accompanists also wear robes for the above three reasons. Jill has seen directors in particular who insist on wearing business suits rather than robes, and she feels this detracts from the unity of the choir.

Instrument Maintenance

Jill looked around the choir room. It was almost hard to imagine how discouraged she had felt several weeks ago. Now she could sit at the desk and work, get music from orderly files, and look forward to conducting the choir in their clean robes in the fall. Oops! What about that out-of-tune piano?

First Jill checks if there are any tuning or maintenance contracts in the music files. To be on the safe side, she also checks with the church secretary and the trustees. She discovers that the church's pipe organ is on a twice-yearly tuning and maintenance contract but that nothing is set for the pianos in the church. Checking with the pastor, Jill discovers that keeping all the church's pianos in working order does fall under her job description.

Since Jill doesn't have a piano herself and therefore knows no tuners, she calls the church organist, who also teaches piano. Sharon gives her the name and the telephone number of a reliable tuner and a second name for back-up. Jill walks through the church to check which rooms have pianos and also asks which are used (by Sunday school, youth, men's and women's organizations, Bible study, or other groups using the church building). She also checks that pianos are not up against heaters or registers, something that church staff often overlook.

Jill calls the tuner as early as possible in the summer, guessing (correctly) that tuners might be busy as fall comes and schools get ready to start. She makes arrangements for the tuner to come when someone will be in the church building who can direct the tuner to the location of all the pianos in the building. She also mentions any specific repair problems (keys that stick or do not sound, broken pedals or hammers) and confirms that the tuner will leave a bill that is payable within thirty days. (Jill is already learning that church bills take awhile to travel the payment route, so she is careful to alert vendors to that fact and to process bills as soon as she receives them.)

If Jill were also the handbell director and/or children's choir director she would be responsible for getting those related instruments in shape, too. (See chapters 7 and 8.) Fortunately Jill doesn't have to do any of that, so she gives herself a well-deserved break, props her feet up, has a glass of mineral water, and prays for guidance and strength for the next task!

Chapter Two:
Planning for the Rehearsal and for Worship

"Sunday comes twice a week."

W hen choir rehearsals begin it feels like Sunday comes twice a week in terms of the preparation needed by choir directors. This preparation is essential for both rehearsal time and worship. Planning in large blocks of time will ease the director's mind, facilitate ordering new music, assure preparation time for the accompanist and music librarian, supply bulletin information in a timely fashion, and enable the choir to set and reach their goals.

The Christian (or Liturgical) Year

From growing up in the church Gil feels like he knows about the church year. Let's see, he thinks, Christmas is the first "big day," Easter comes in the spring, then Choir Sunday ends the school year. But the denominational calendar in the choir room lists Advent and Lent and has a confusing variety of colors listed. So Gil schedules a time with Pastor Lee to learn more about this and about the lectionary that Pastor Lee uses in preparing sermons.

"Thanks for coming, Gil," welcomes Pastor Lee as they sit together at a table in the pastor's office. "I'm glad for a chance to explain the church year to you so we can begin to plan worship together. The church year gives us our focus for worship.

"First, let's look at the big picture. The church year has an ebb and flow around the major festivals of Christmas and Easter. These days of Christ's birth and resurrection are each prefaced by a season of preparation.

"Advent, with its four Sundays, is preparation for the coming of Christ in the Incarnation. Some folks begin singing Christmas carols immediately after Thanksgiving, but we try to resist the temptation here at Second Church! Worship in the Advent season focuses on the biblical preparation for Christmas and prepares us for God's gifts. Christmas Eve/Day, along with the following Sunday, celebrates Christ's birth, a high point in the Christian year. Epiphany focuses on the showing of Christ to the Gentiles through the visit of the Magi (Matt. 2:1) and is celebrated on January 6 or the first Sunday of January.

"The season after the Epiphany begins with the Baptism of the Lord, also called the First Sunday After the Epiphany. Depending on the date of Easter, the season after the Epiphany has between three and eight Sundays focusing on Jesus' teachings and mission. This season ends with Transfiguration Sunday, celebrating Jesus' transfiguration on the mountain with Elijah and Moses.

"Lent is the prelude to Easter and encompasses a variety of holy days, beginning with Ash Wednesday, a day of repentance. Five Sundays follow Ash Wednesday in Lent. Palm/Passion Sunday is the sixth Sunday in Lent, with the celebration of Jesus' ride into Jerusalem and the foreshadowing of the Last Supper and Crucifixion, since many of the congregation do not attend the Maundy Thursday and Good Friday services. Many churches are also beginning to recapture the ancient tradition of the Easter Vigil. Akin to Christmas Eve, this is a service of scriptures and songs, darkness and light, leading up to the Easter morning discovery of resurrection. Let's think about including it this spring, Gil.

"Easter, the second high point of the Christian year, is followed by seven Sundays of Easter, all celebrating the resurrection and resurrection appearances of Jesus. On the Thursday before the Seventh Sunday of Easter the less familiar holy day of the Ascension occurs. This is when Jesus' resurrection appearances ended and he ascended into heaven (Luke 24:44-53). The time between Easter and Pentecost is also called 'the great fifty days.'

"Pentecost is the birthday of the church, when the Holy Spirit descended and the disciples were empowered. It often gets lost in Memorial Day and graduate recognition, but its loss is a loss for Christians in celebrating and claiming the Holy Spirit and the birth of the Church, so we make sure that Pentecost stays on our calendar here at Second Church," remarked Pastor Lee.

"The season after Pentecost begins with the celebration of Trinity Sunday, and continues through summer into fall. This season includes the special Sundays of World Communion (first Sunday in October), All Saints' Day (November 1 or the first Sunday in November), and Thanksgiving. This season ends with Reign of Christ/Christ the King Sunday, as the last Sunday before Advent."

By talking through the calendar with Pastor Lee, Gil began to see where different anthems could fit during Advent, Lent, and the season after Epiphany, for example. This will give his planning focus.

Other Special Sundays

Pastor Lee continued, "Every denomination also observes other occasions. The United Methodist Church, for example, has provisions for special Sundays within the liturgical year: Human Relations Day, One Great Hour of Sharing, Native American Awareness, Heritage, Golden Cross, Peace with Justice, Christian Education, Rural Life, Student Day, and Aldersgate. Secular holidays are sometimes celebrated in individual churches as well: Martin Luther King, Jr. Day, Boy Scout or Girl Scout Sunday, Festival of the Christian Home, Mother's Day, Memorial Day, Father's Day, Independence Day, Labor Day, and Reformation Day. When adding additional special Sundays, it is important to honor the flow of the liturgical year and to focus on the events of Christ's life and the things that make us Christian. This is something that we work through in our worship committee meetings, which I hope you will be able to attend the first Tuesday of each month, Gil," Pastor Lee added.

"I'll try to make those meetings," replied Gil. "Tell me, what is the lectionary? It is mentioned here in next month's newsletter for each Sunday."

The Lectionary

Pastor Lee replied, "To facilitate following the liturgical year many churches use a lectionary or schedule of scripture readings.

This schedule is spread over three years and encompasses most of the Bible, with readings for each Sunday and holy day from the Old Testament, Psalms, Gospels, and Epistles (the letters of the New Testament). Each of the three years focuses on one Gospel: Year A on Matthew, Year B on Mark, and Year C on Luke. The Gospel of John is parceled out over the three years. During the Sundays of Easter, Acts replaces the Old Testament reading. Generally the Gospel readings follow the liturgical year (seasons of the church) and during all seasons except Pentecost the Old Testament and Psalm readings are correlated to the Gospel lesson.

"Using the lectionary helps everyone here to plan ahead for each service by providing specific scriptures for each week. I may decide to lift up certain readings in the sermon (Gospel one week, Old Testament the next); still, using the lectionary guarantees that over time the congregation will be exposed to the entirety of the Bible," finished Pastor Lee.

Topical Preaching

Meanwhile in another city, Jill and Rev. John had also talked through the church year. Rev. John continued, "I prefer to do what is called topical preaching, preaching on a certain topic each week or preaching a series of sermons around a topic. I try not to limit the congregation's exposure to scripture by using certain favorite scriptures of mine repeatedly; but I do feel it is helpful for the congregation to focus on a particular topic of importance for the community. I will try to plan my topical preaching in advance so that you can coordinate anthems. I have a copy of the scriptures and themes for September through December for you here, Jill. It is possible that they will change if a different topic becomes more urgent, but I will let you know as soon as I am able."

Worship Planning

"Thank you all for coming to our worship committee meeting tonight. We are particularly glad to welcome our new choir director, Gil. Gil, I believe you know everyone here?"

"Yes, thank you. I'm glad to be here."

"I want to remind us about some basic principles as we begin our planning tonight," Sue, the worship chairperson, continued.

"Whether lectionary or topical preaching is used, the worship service should tie together in themes and mood. This is not to say that one idea is represented in five different ways and called worship. Rather, the scriptures, sermon, prayers, hymns, and anthem do not contradict one another, but flow together and center the worshipers in praise and in the presence of God.

"This takes coordination between pastor, musicians, and other worship planners. Here at Second Church we plan worship monthly, planning for October in September, and so on. Detailed planning can be accomplished this way. Gil, I understand you are already working on October anthems with your choir. Have you and Pastor Lee talked about the lectionary and how it guides our planning?" Seeing Gil nod, Sue went on, "We try in these meetings to focus on the details: hymns, anthems, prayers, visuals, laity involvement, and movement. Now let's get started on World Communion Sunday, the first Sunday in October."

At Rev. John's church, Jill attended worship committee during the last week of August. She was welcomed by the chairperson, Millard, who began the meeting with prayer and then explained, "Here at Hope Church we use quarterly worship planning sessions. We focus on the seasons of the church year. We're getting a head start planning Advent/Christmas/Epiphany now. Our November meeting will focus on the season after the Epiphany. We'll plan Lent through Eastertide during January, and for the Pentecost season in March. Notice that we avoid planning during December (Christmas) and April (Easter), because we know everyone is extra busy then."

Millard continued, "Rev. John usually plans the scriptures and themes prior to our meetings so we can each do some preliminary planning before our meetings." Jill noted the meeting times and seasons in her calendar and then blocked out time before and after each meeting for her own planning.

Planning and Setting Goals for the Choir Year

Jill sat in on a session about "Planning for the Choir Year" at a late-summer workshop, and listened to the leader, Tom, explain: "As a choir director you will find it most helpful to plan your anthems in large blocks. Summertime, when most choirs aren't rehearsing, is a good time to look at the year ahead. Blessed are you if your pastor preaches by the lectionary or lets you know her or his scripture and themes or foci at least three months ahead!

"Before you begin planning, take some time to consider your goals for the choir in the upcoming year. Yours may be strictly to survive but it will help you and the choir to grow if you set some reachable and tangible goals." Jill thought of the myriad of her own goals as she began to work with the choir, and vowed to pick three goals from her list to work on earnestly.

Director's Goals
• Carry out well-planned rehearsals.
• Become comfortable with beat patterns.
• Attend a church music workshop.
• Learn one new anthem each season.
• Attend a Bible study class.
• Compose an introit for the choir.
• Get two volunteers to help with odd jobs.
• Learn to direct the "Hallelujah" chorus.
• Improve cutoffs or entrance cues in conducting.
• Lighten up rehearsals with an extra smile.

Tom continued, "You will also want to consider some goals for your choir. These are some of the things I could work on with my own choir this year. And no, I don't have a perfect choir yet!" Tom admitted, to the laughter of the workshop participants.

Choir's Goals
• Improve the choreography of the processional.
• Watch the director carefully for cutoffs or entrances.

- Extend each section's range by one note in each direction.
- Be able to sing one anthem *a cappella*.
- Be able to sing one anthem in mixed formation (not sections).
- Learn one *Messiah* chorus.
- Achieve better diction.
- Spend less time talking during rehearsals.
- Work for a better soft (*piano*) sound.
- Work on better breath support.
- Include sectional rehearsals to improve singing.

Choosing Anthems

"Any questions so far?" Tom asked.

"I have one," said Gil. "How do you know what the choir can sing? I have a new piece I am excited about. It has a great text, wonderful music, and would fit in perfectly with the pastor's sermon focus. But how do I know if my choir can sing it?"

"Good question," Tom said. "You will become a better judge of this as your experience increases, but here are a few guidelines."

1. If you can learn it, you can teach it. (Conversely, if you do not know it, there is very little chance that your choir will be able to sing it!)
2. Can you sing each vocal part? This learning will give you some idea about how long it will take your singers to learn it, if they will be able to sight-read it, and if they will need sectional rehearsals.
3. Do the parts fit within the range of your singers, or will they fit reasonably well after you have worked on extending the singers' ranges in a number of rehearsals?
4. Is the accompaniment within the technical skills of your accompanist or is there a difficult spot that might be simplified? Please don't do this simplification more than once in a great while. Be certain to give the accompanist the piece far enough in advance for him or her to work out those spots, and if necessary help them get some lessons to develop their skills. Beware of constantly having the accompaniment bear all the interest and difficulty of a piece. Some pieces are very easy and almost boring for the choir because the accompaniment has all the interest.

5. Will it take a reasonable amount of rehearsal time? If it takes three entire rehearsals to learn one piece, you have lost valuable time for the other pieces the choir needs to sing. If the piece can be well learned over a period of six to eight weeks, spending fifteen to twenty minutes on it each week, it may be worth the time and effort. (This long-term learning is much more valuable than short-term cramming, in addition to being more fun!)

"If you think the effort of learning this piece is worth it, be sure that you perform it again reasonably soon, so that it becomes part of your permanent repertoire. This may have seemed like a long answer to your brief question, Gil, but the music you pick will flavor your worship services and involve your choir's voices and minds for good or bad over this next year. These are important choices that you make," Tom emphasized.

The Christian Year and Choir Planning

"Now, as you look at the year as a whole, remember the liturgical year. Sometimes I start with Christmas and Easter. If you sing two anthems on these days it's often good to use one familiar and one new. Plan for any special services: cantatas, *Messiah* selections, or services of Lessons and Carols now available in many worship books.

"Be certain to stay within the seasonal emphasis. Performing your choir's Christmas cantata the first Sunday of Advent can skip over our spiritual preparation for Christmas. Note that Lessons and Carols services and even some *Messiah* selections focus on the prophecies about Jesus' birth and can be very appropriate during Advent. The same issue arises during Lent. Many cantatas focus on Easter morning and, when performed on Palm/Passion Sunday or during Lent, omit our journey toward Easter. The choir can help teach the congregation more about these seasons and the stories of the church by focusing on the themes of Lent and Advent, leading the church to better and deeper understandings of Easter and Christmas by their preparation," finished Tom.

Sitting Down to Plan

After the worship meeting and workshop, Gil spends some time planning for the choir year. He begins with the denominational calendar of seasons and holidays that lists the scripture readings for each day. Like Jill, Gil also has the church's planning calendar. Gil marks these dates on the choir room calendar.

It might seem that only those events that apply to the music program should be noted on the choir room calendar. But as Gil will quickly learn, all church activities are interrelated. Many choir members are involved in other church events, and extra rehearsals cannot be scheduled on those times. Knowing that the seniors group is taking a trip over a certain Sunday may warn Gil that senior choir members may be absent that week. When the church hosts a group of homeless persons, that time may contain different commitments for choir members, as well as focusing worship on the Sundays around the experience. Even rummage sales can affect choir personnel and rehearsal spaces.

Whether the church is large or small, turf battles can develop over calendar items. Gil is well advised to note dates as he receives them, as well as getting choir times on the church calendar as soon as possible. (This includes special choir parties, even if they are "closed" events for choir members only. Otherwise you may get overscheduled with potentially conflicting events.)

Gil now has a number of guiding principles from his talk with Pastor Lee, the worship committee meeting, and the workshop he attended. He begins to fill in anthem suggestions.

- something familiar for the choir's first Sunday back
- seasonal theme guidelines
- holiday pieces, which may require extended rehearsal
- scripture references to coordinate with scriptural anthems
- variety of music (fast/slow, energetic/meditative, praise/ inspirational, easy and fun/challenging, favorites of choir/congregation/pastor/director, contemporary/classical, hymn-based/free-form, four-part/unison/two-part, solos/ instruments, familiar/new, meeting choir's goals/director's goals)

One of the other resources Gil uses in his planning is his church's hymnal. He has found a wealth of hymn materials by using the indexes at the back of the hymnal. Most often he uses the scripture or seasonal indexes, to coordinate with the lectionary or seasonal themes. In some hymnals he has found indexes for introits, benedictions, and children's music. All of these aid Gil in finding service music or less familiar hymns that can be used as anthems.

Gil will pencil in his choices as he goes week by week, then he will go back and look at the overall picture for balance, particularly noting that he has not scheduled more difficult or new music than rehearsal time allows. Most choirs are willing to attend an extra rehearsal or two for special presentations but will expect you (the director) to honor the weekly time commitment and cut-off.

Gil will find it helpful to plan like this about twice a year, for September through December, and for January through June. If he is inspired and has time, sketching in some pieces throughout the entire year will help in planning ahead. Gil wants to avoid the pitfall of planning each week as he comes to rehearsal and finding himself directing the same sort of pieces over and over. This does not mean that things will not occasionally change—your one and only tenor ends up in the hospital for a month, the pastor needs to change themes to deal with an urgent crisis in the congregation, ordered music does not arrive on time. But Gil writes his choices in pencil and has a plan with which to work. Printing up a "proposed schedule" for the choir helps them to see their progress and gives them pieces to look forward to. Make sure the church secretary receives a copy for the bulletin, too, with titles and composers' names.

Ordering New Music

Once Gil has laid out his September through December schedule he can order any new music needed. He is careful to remember to count the director and accompanist, as well as choir members, and to add a few extra copies for choir growth and music loss.

At the summer workshop Gil learned about a discount music

house in his area. He calls them to set up an account for the church, and asks that all music be sent to his attention. He also checks with the church treasurer on Second Church's policy for paying bills. When the bill is received Gil documents receipt of the music and then sends the bill on to the treasurer for payment. When he bought music at the workshop he kept the receipt, filled out a "voucher form" kept in the church office, and sent that to the church treasurer for reimbursement.

Although the treasurer keeps a running tally of expenditures for each department, Gil keeps track also in the choir room. He doesn't want to get ready to order Christmas music and find there are no budget monies left for the year. When the music comes Gil will check that it is what he ordered and then pass it on to the choir librarian. (See chapter 1.)

Balancing Multiple Choirs and Services

Over at Hope Church Jill has an additional complication in her planning, which makes scheduling the music like a logic problem.

1. Hope Church has two services each week.
2. The adult choir, which Jill directs, sings regularly at the second service, and once a month at the early service.
3. The bell choir plays once a month at the second service.
4. The children's choir generally sings at the first service, except on the Sunday before Christmas and on Mother's Day when they sing at both services.
5. The pastor has requested that there be a choir or special music at every service.

Jill ends up with a diagram like this:

SUNDAY	1st	2nd	3rd	4th	5th
1.	Adult Choir	Instrumental Solo	Children's Choir	Vocal Solo	Organ Solo
2.	Adult Choir	Adult Choir	Adult Choir and Bells	Adult Choir	Adult Choir

This diagram gives her a place to begin and also enables the various choirs to keep track of when they sing. December and May will change slightly to accommodate the special singing of the children's choir. It helps all concerned to have this kind of schedule rather than to have the children's and bell choirs wait to perform "when they're ready." This way everyone has clear goals and can plan ahead according to scriptures and seasons, and a soloist and instrumentalist can be involved each month as well.

Planning Individual Rehearsals

Within each rehearsal, Gil will try to balance the levels of challenge for the choir as well as the mood and vocal ranges of the pieces. He begins with prayer, vocal warm-ups, the hymns and service music for the coming Sunday, then while energy is still high tackles the major choral problem for the week. Sunday's anthem receives adequate review, and future anthems are rehearsed following Gil's careful preparations, working ahead for the next four to six weeks. Gil keeps his energy up to motivate the choir. By modeling good posture and eye contact, he encourages the choir to do the same.

Gil understands that working through the problems that each piece presents gives the choir a sense of accomplishment. There is no "let's sing through that once more" without a goal in mind. Mindless singing has no place in Gil's choir rehearsals. Before singing an anthem or section of an anthem he reminds the choir of the essential ingredients of that piece, often with just a word or phrase: "diction," "phrasing," "breathe deeply," "*molto legato*," "remember the repeat."

Gil keeps the pace of the rehearsal moving, without anxious pressure. His goals for himself and the choir guide him. There is room for occasional laughter, and also time for sharing the personal concerns of choir members during a special time of the rehearsal. When rehearsal is over, Gil and the choir members have a sense of accomplishment from having worked hard and made beautiful music.

Gil's careful preparation is one part of creating successful rehearsals. Others include:

1. Adequate preparation and sensitivity to the overall direction of the rehearsal on the part of the accompanist
2. The preparation of the choir librarian in having music ready
3. The rehearsal space itself—good lighting and ventilation, comfortable temperature, appropriate chairs for singers, clear sight lines for everyone to see the director

Gil models Christian cooperation in working with the accompanist and librarian, and is gracious in his appreciation of them both publicly and privately. If the tempo or other aspects of a piece are different from what is marked in the music, Gil works them out with the accompanist before the rehearsal.

Gil gives the Sunday morning warm-up time equal preparation, because it is in essence a "mini-rehearsal." On Sunday morning he sets the spiritual tone, warms up voices, and reviews the music for the service, giving verbal reminders before singing. This time is short, as people come breathless from Sunday school or getting children ready. Gil works to frame the musical experience so that the choir can lead in worship with voice and spirit.

Chapter Three:
Processing and Recessing

"Why don't they teach 'choir choreography' at those workshops?"

Jill had enough things at Hope Church to occupy her time and energy for the first several months. She knew that the choir's procession during the opening hymn was ragged, but they did all end up where they were supposed to be, so she left it alone.

Before the January worship committee meeting Jill received a call from Millard, the chairperson, asking if they could talk about the history of processions in the meeting and then discuss some ideas he had for the use of processions at their church. Millard also asked if Jill would invite the children's choir director, Grace, and the hand-bell choir director, David, to the January worship meeting. Because Millard framed the "processional question" within worship not as a problem, but as an important part of the movement in worship, Jill felt encouraged to work with him.

The Adult Choir

After the greeting and opening prayer by Rev. John, Millard opened the worship committee meeting by saying, "I would like us to think together today about movement in worship, about how our bodies are involved and how we enact the journeys of Christians. We are a 'moving' people from the time of the Exodus, through the Palm Sunday parade, to the final days when all of earth's peoples will process to worship God (as told in Isaiah 2:2-3). We move individually, as we stand to praise while singing, and sit for prayers and listening. We move together into worship and out to service, to the table for Communion, to the font for baptism, and to the altar with our offerings. Getting the choirs, acolytes, and clergy to their appointed places each week is a practical matter, but it also sets the tone for our worship.

"I have been wondering if we might suspend the choral processing during Lent to 'mark' the season, to draw people's attention to it as different from the season after the Epiphany, which will be ending. Then when we use a procession for Palm Sunday its impact will be higher since it will be special. Jill, I think you have some concerns about the choir's part of the processional?"

"Yes, Millard, I do. I like the idea of not always processing. It will be nice during Lent to be able to quietly enter the choir loft before the prelude begins and to be able to intentionally listen to it. Two of the older women in the choir really have a difficult time managing the steps into the chancel during the procession. We have shortened all the robes this year so that they do not cause a problem with the steps. And Steve puts the music folders in the choir loft before worship for those who can't manage the weight of folders and hymnals in procession. What other things do you think would improve our processions?"

Mary spoke up. "Processions bother me sometimes. I like to hear the singing of the choir as it comes forward, but it is disheartening when they don't seem to know the hymn. I don't like it when things look too military, with heavy steps and sharp right turns. It seems to me that a procession can look graceful without looking too casual."

"I think the gracefulness that Mary mentioned is important," Millard said. "If you know we're going to make the Palm Sunday procession important, Jill, can you take some time in rehearsals to work on it? I'm thinking about things like the partners staying together, the choir knowing the hymn well so they can help lead the congregation and not be distracted by the processing, and spacing the procession so that as the choir moves into the chancel they don't get bunched up."

"Thanks, Millard. It's helpful to have some specific things to work on. Do you think it distracts if Millie and June enter from the front and slip into the loft as the choir enters during a processional? June especially feels uncomfortable processing."

"I don't see anything wrong with that. People are focused on their singing and on the procession, and if that helps June and Millie feel more comfortable, do it," replied Millard.

"One thing I would like to consider," volunteered Rev. John, "is having the choir move occasionally to the middle of the chancel to sing. You know, the congregation really enjoys seeing the choir better, but it can take a long time to get everyone in and out of the loft. Could we do that sometime in a less formal service, or when we don't have the extra length with Communion or baptism? Is it possible for the choir to practice that movement so they know where they're going and how to get back to their spots in the loft?"

Jill thought a moment. "On Mother's Day we're doing a particularly lively anthem with piano accompaniment. That might be a good time to move the choir out of the loft to sing. And if we plan to do it after Easter, I can plan time to rehearse that movement, after we shape up our processional for Palm Sunday and Easter. How does that sound?"

"I think that will fit well in that service. Then if it goes well, let's consider doing it more often," agreed Rev. John.

"What about recessing?" asked Mike. "It seems unfinished to me when the choir processes but doesn't recess. Is there any special reason the choir doesn't recess?"

"To be honest," replied Jill, "I've been so busy trying to learn how to direct the choir that I never even thought about recessing. I see what you mean about it balancing the service. Have the rest of you missed it?"

"Well, it was on my list to discuss," admitted Millard. "We all appreciate the great job you've been doing with the choir, Jill, so we didn't want to add anything extra. But it seems to me that when we process we should recess. Now during Lent we won't process, so we won't recess. But on Palm Sunday and Easter let's plan a recession also. Can you work with the choir to assure that the last person will be leaving the sanctuary as we finish the hymn? Last year the choir always started out as soon as the hymn began and then the congregation was left without choir support at the end of the hymn. It was a letdown. If you can time how many stanzas it will take the choir to recess, then leave in the middle of the hymn when you need to, that would be great."

The Children's Choir

Mike spoke up, "Since Grace is here I wanted to mention the last time the children sang. During the procession, it was cute but distracting, to see the younger children who didn't seem to know what was happening. Do you practice the procession with the children in the sanctuary, Grace? Would you like some parental help during the practice or in worship?"

"We do come up to the sanctuary to practice the procession before we sing in worship each time," replied Grace. "With all the excitement at Christmas, some of the younger children did get confused last time, but I think that will settle down. I have wondered if it would help to pair the younger children with older children during the procession. What do you think? It would look different from the way we usually do it, by height."

"I think it goes back to gracefulness again," Millard said. "If the height isn't exactly graduated, but the children move smoothly, I think that is what is important. I think people understand about the problems getting the children up front, Grace, so don't spend your whole time worrying about it in rehearsal."

"Grace, I notice you had Yvonne help the children with finding their places for the anthem time during Advent, and that went much smoother than in November," commented Rev. John.

Grace smiled. "That was Yvonne's idea, and I think it worked well. She or another parent will help the children find their places in the chancel when we sing each time from now on."

"Grace," Mary spoke up, "there is another thing I've heard praised in connection with the children this year. Last year whenever they sang in worship there were loud noises in the hallway before service. This year it has been wonderfully quiet. How do you do it?"

"I'm glad that someone noticed," laughed Grace. "I've worked harder this fall on the children's 'worship behavior' and preparing them for leadership in worship. We begin our procession in the choir room, sort of a follow-the-leader, and try to see how quietly we can enter the service. The children have really gotten into the spirit of it, especially since we leave the choir room with a prayer."

The Handbell Choir

"David, you've been rather quiet this evening," invited Millard. "I know the handbell choir doesn't ring every Sunday and when you do ring, it is often the prelude. I have to admit I usually come into worship during the middle of your prelude. Do you have any questions or ideas to share with this committee?"

"I guess I just wonder if anyone has any concerns regarding the handbell choir. Because of the positions of the bell tables our entrances and exits have much less room for change or variation. One of the things the handbell choir saw at another concert during December that we hope to try here next Advent is a procession with handbells where we would play while coming down the aisle. It was very effective as an introduction and accompaniment to the opening hymn at the concert at Second Church."

"I like that idea of a handbell procession. I saw one at my sister's church last Easter and it was beautiful," affirmed Mary.

"I'm usually ushering when the handbells play," said Mike. "I like the way you all enter with your gloves on and your music ready to play. Everyone files in in order and goes right to their place. It helps me focus on the music because I know that you are focused on the music."

"I'm glad you feel that way," nodded David. "Especially since we usually play the prelude, we feel it's important to help set the mood for the service."

Moving to Other Spaces

"I have one other idea I'd like to bring before this committee," said Jill. "I know we're focusing this meeting on Lent and Easter, but I would like to do something a little different for Pentecost, and I would like the input of this committee. The anthem I would like to do has beautiful vocal parts and uses the scripture about the coming of the Spirit. I thought it might be particularly effective if the choir stood around the edges of the sanctuary, surrounding the congregation. I think people could really feel the coming of the Spirit if we sang it that way. The choir may be a little shy about doing it, but if this committee feels it could add to our worship, that would help me encourage the choir."

"I think it's great that you are willing to try some new ways of presenting anthems, Jill," affirmed Rev. John. "Pentecost is a good time to try something like that. Will the choir be able to see you? What about the organist?"

"The anthem is unaccompanied, so the organ isn't a problem. I thought maybe an usher could move down the box we use occasionally with the massed choirs for me to stand on. And, of course, I'll need to practice the choir moving out to those spots from the loft. Or they could sit among the congregation at the ends of the pews near where they'll sing."

"I think the idea is good, Jill," replied Millard. "Why don't we work out the details at our next meeting. Do take it to the choir as an idea that the worship committee encourages. I see you all nodding in agreement, so let's move on to the details for Ash Wednesday."

Chapter Four:
The Budget

"How do we get what we need?"

Yearly Budgets

One of the real "finds" Gil made when going through the choir room desk was a page listing the expenses for the previous year. This gave him a place to start when the finance committee asked him in September for his budget for the coming year. The page read:

- Organ Maintenance (yearly contract)
- Piano Tuning (all pianos in church yearly, sanctuary and choir room pianos twice a year)
- Handbell Maintenance and Supplies
- Orff/Children's Choir Instruments (maintenance)
- Chancel Choir Music (anthems, cantatas)
- Handbell Choir Music
- Children's Choir Music
- Youth Choir Music
- Organ Music
- Robe Cleaning (all choirs)
- Soloists and Instrumentalists (summer or special services)
- Periodicals and Professional Memberships
- Supplies (office and music)
- Continuing Education for Directors and Accompanists
- Guest Musicians (to lead choir workshops)
- Music Publicity and Mailings (fall recruitment, special programs, birthdays)
- Sound System (tape players and cassettes that are used exclusively by the choirs, as opposed to sanctuary sound systems)

On the second page, the former director included a breakdown of estimated costs for some additional items.

• Five new anthems for January through June at $1.10 per anthem for each choir member plus five (director, accompanist, extras for future and loss)
• Four new anthems for September through December at $1.10 per anthem for each choir member plus five
• One new cantata for December at $6.95 for each choir member plus ten (we always have extra singers at cantata time)

Breakdowns were also given for the children and youth choir music budgets, figuring the number of anthems and amounts. Handbells were listed too:

Handbell Maintenance and Supplies:
• Gloves
• Polishing Supplies
• Repairs
• Replacement Folders
• Music Stands
• Table Covers and Pads

Periodicals and professional memberships were listed with current or projected costs for each per year. Gil knew that there was one periodical in conjunction with a membership for each choir, and one denominational music magazine.

Continuing education was estimated also, listing costs for short workshops as well as a longer workshop.

Further searching through the desk turned up treasurer's reports, which listed actual expenses to date. Gil noticed that the former director had overspent on the anthems from January through June, but that monies were still available in the continuing education part of the budget. That gave him some leeway to purchase new anthems between now and Christmas.

Gil used last year's budget as his basis for estimating this year's budget, adding for increased anthem costs and memberships. He also needed to figure in more copies for the children's and adult choirs, which had each added five new members over the year. Since the handbell choir had purchased new table pads and covers that would last several years, Gil shifted those funds to the handbell music line. More music would be required, as the handbell choir planned to go to a festival in the coming year. When he submitted the new budget to the finance committee, he included a paragraph at the end explaining these increases and shifts.

Fund Raising

Later that month Gil met with two members from the handbell choir to begin planning their trip to a regional handbell festival. Carol brought the brochure from the sponsoring organization and her estimate of the registration and room and board costs for the choir to attend. Jim had met with the pastor and finance chairperson to discuss the possibilities for fund raising. After Carol shared the total funds needed, Jim told about his meeting.

"Right now Pastor Lee is reluctant to take any extra offerings, due to the use of extra offerings for mission work. Sally suggests that any fund raising avoid the months of November (church-wide stewardship campaign) and April (the women's group spring bazaar). I explained the value of this trip for our choir in building skills as well as fellowship, and both Pastor Lee and Sally agreed that this seems like a worthwhile project. In the last church she served, Pastor Lee's choirs were planning a trip and held a concert that raised a lot of money. Sally suggested that our church hasn't had many dinners lately and that a fund-raising dinner could both raise money and bring some added fellowship to the church."

"I'm glad nobody mentioned candy sales," laughed Gil. "I'm worn out on those from school."

"I was talking with Karen yesterday," said Carol. "She had an idea about 'ringing Valentines.' People would purchase a Valentine for a friend, and the bell choir (or several of us) could go to their home to ring on Valentine's Day for, say, five minutes. She's seen it done before with singers. Could it work with ringers?"

"You know, I'm very willing to begin baking sourdough bread again as a fund raiser. That raised about $400 for the children's choir robes last year," volunteered Jim.

"I've missed your bread, Jim," said Gil. "Let's count on that as part of our strategy. Do you two want to discuss these ideas more or are we ready to take them to the choir for discussion on Wednesday?"

Payment Procedures

Meanwhile, over at Hope Church, Jill sat down to deal with the organ tuner's bill, which had been submitted several months ago. "I've got to get this bill paid!" she thought. The first step was to find out the procedure from the pastor or church secretary and then be sure to keep a running tally of monies spent. Some churches just need the director's initials on the bill as authorization. Others ask the musician to fill out a voucher form and submit it to the church secretary or treasurer. Before submitting the bill, Jill made sure that the music files included the name, address, and phone number of the technician so that she had quick access to it in an organ emergency. Jill vowed to stay on top of bill paying; it assists the church treasurer and the vendor, and avoids late fees.

More Fund Raising

Later that week, Jill brought Marvin and Grace to the administrative council, after asking the chairperson to put them on the agenda.

"As you may have heard," began Jill, "we are considering getting new robes for the children's choir. Marvin's brought one of the current robes to show you why we need new ones." Marvin held up a faded robe, with sagging zipper, and frayed cuffs.

Grace spoke next. "At the choir parents meeting we discussed the robes, and what we would like to have for the children. We're looking at a color that would blend with the other choirs and the sanctuary, and we're looking at fabric that would stand up better to use by children."

"We have discussed various fund-raising methods, but a lot of the parents feel worn out on fund raising between the schools and scouts and sports. So we decided to come to the council to ask for help," said Marvin.

"The music department has not used all of our budget for this current year," Jill shared. "And Grace is willing to cut back on the children's choir purchases next year. We feel that the instruments are sufficient for now and that there are many pieces in the library and in our new hymnal for the children to sing. I am willing to also cut two anthems from the budget if needed."

"Whoa," laughed Pat, the chairperson. "We can certainly see that the children need new robes. I'm surprised we didn't notice the awful state of the robes before. We're always so glad to hear the children sing, we probably didn't notice the robes. I'm glad the three of you brought it to our attention. Since we're just setting the budget for next year, can we include some money from the council rather than slicing the music budget?"

Harry spoke up. "As finance chairperson for our successful stewardship drive (cheers!), I think that we can cover some of the cost. Could the rest either be picked up by the music budget or raised another way?"

Rev. John broke in, "You know, we haven't had any special offerings for a while. I wonder if we might designate two Sundays when people could contribute to the new children's choir robes?"

"I'd certainly be glad to buy a new robe for my grandchild," said Roy, "and I'm sure others would be glad to help also."

Pat took charge. "So perhaps we should designate the first two Sundays of next month as a time to contribute for new children's choir robes. Then at our next meeting we would know how much we still need from the council or the music budget. Does that sound agreeable? Does someone want to make a motion?"

Chapter Five:
Managing Your Time

"Where did the day go?" or "Things that can eat up your time if you let them"

Meetings

Gil had been surprised to find out in his meeting with Pastor Lee (in chapter 2) that he was expected to attend monthly worship meetings, but he guessed correctly that these were important meetings for him. He was surprised again when the secretary at Second Church called early one morning to remind him about the weekly staff meeting he had not heard about. The mail in his box on Sunday had requested his presence at finance this month for budget setting and at trustees next month for discussion of the pipe organ. There was also a note requesting him to provide music for the men's monthly breakfast. Where was he to find all this time for meetings, in addition to his rehearsals and planning? But if he didn't find the time, how would he stay in touch with the church and its leaders, and defend the music program?

Luckily for Gil, his friend at Fourth Church called to ask about borrowing copies of an anthem for her choir. "Oh, Gloria, I am so glad you called. You have been directing choirs for a long time now, tell me what to do. I'm getting notices to attend more meetings than I have time for, and they all seem important. How do you manage meetings?"

Gloria chuckled. "You're right, I have learned something about this. When I was at Faith Church they nearly 'meetinged' me to death! Rev. John and I worked together there and we had a good talk about where meetings fit into the musician's schedule. He helped me to remember my priorities.

"You were asked to direct the choirs at Second Church, right?" Gloria went on. "That means your choir preparation comes first. The meetings you attend should help you enable the choir's work. The important thing about the church leaders is letting them know you're on their side, that you're there to help build up the whole church. If you're cooperative and communicative about your work and can be open to their ideas too, then you can miss some meetings here and there."

"Well, what about finance and trustees?" asked Gil.

"I try to submit my budget early to the finance chairperson with an explanation on any changes from the previous year. That gives her time to talk with me before the meeting if she has any questions. I only go to the meeting if I'm worried about a particular request that is new or different. I try to stay on or under budget, so I don't expect pressure from the finance committee. Sometimes I go to the trustees meeting if I am the only person who has the information they need, but I try to make sure that doesn't happen! It's always good to have another choir person in the know.

"Some years I've had a music committee, a small group of persons with whom I had lunch or coffee after choir every six weeks and who understood my goals for the music program. Then any one of those persons could represent the music ministry at any church meeting. Right now I have a choir whose members are very active in church committees. If a meeting is coming up where music input needs to be made and I can't go, I ask the choir member on that committee to represent me, to take my ideas and information and to report back to me after the meeting. That works for my style, which gives the choir members themselves a lot of ownership of the program. I can't say what will work for you, but I know you're working hard, trying to communicate and be open. Your choir is beginning to feel your support of them. That support will come back to you in the church, and you will feel like you're working with the whole church, not like you have to defend the music program."

"Thanks, Gloria. Do you have staff meetings at Fourth Church? And do you go each week?"

"Yes, we do have them," said Gloria. "And no, I don't always go. The staff meeting used to be the place where the pastor did her worship planning and so I had to be there. Now that we're using the worship committee for worship planning, the staff meeting is a time just to keep in touch. I try to go about half the time, and the weeks I don't go I make sure I touch base with everyone sometime during that week. Usually all I need to do is stop and say 'Hi! How are you doing?'" (See also chapter 9.)

"Thanks for sharing your thoughts and support, Gloria," replied Gil. "You've earned the anthem copies this time!"

Time Management and Choirs

Jill was determined that the beautiful choir room she had worked so hard to uncover (in chapter 1) would stay that way. She was delighted to see that Lillian took a few minutes immediately after each rehearsal to pick up any extra music lying around. On Sundays Lillian had left a folder on the piano for the anthem to be filed away by choir members as part of their after-service time, when they hung up their robes. That managed the music part of it. Sam, ever helpful, kept an eye on the chairs and pencils, both before and after rehearsal. Jill made a note to thank them publicly in the church newsletter; Thanksgiving time seems appropriate, she thought. I'm certainly thankful I don't have to spend time cleaning up after rehearsals.

Jill's own rehearsal preparations, aided by her overall planning done in the summer, consisted of sitting down each week in a time slot between Sunday and rehearsal day to make a detailed rehearsal schedule. She planned the order of the anthems to warm up the choir, took advantage of the beginning energy of the rehearsal for musical challenges, allowed for less strenuous anthems at the end of rehearsal, had an ebb and flow of tempi and vocal ranges, and included devotions, warm-ups, upcoming hymns, and announcement time. Jill had scheduled the things she did every week in logical time slots, and filled in the anthems according to their challenges and goals as they varied from week to week.

This detailed planning seemed to get easier as Jill learned more about how she and the choir worked together, recognized the places in the anthems that would take special care, and gained confidence in her ability to conduct an effective rehearsal. This confidence did not rule out planning altogether, for Jill had sat through too many rehearsals with the former director when he had obviously not planned ahead and when the singers grew frustrated.

Between rehearsal and Sunday Jill spent less than a half hour making notes for the next rehearsal from the previous rehearsal's progress, getting her own music in order for Sunday, and following up on absences. Jill had learned something useful from the previous director—keeping a sign-out sheet in an obvious place in the choir room. The sign-out sheet was marked with all rehearsal and performance dates and choir members understood that it was their responsibility to sign out when they planned to be absent.

June took attendance each week and left the list on the choir room desk. Jill compared the attendance sheet and sign-out sheet, then called those who were absent without signing out, to check on them and remind them about Sunday's anthem and warm-up time. Jill knew choirs who didn't let absentees sing on Sunday if they missed rehearsal, but her choir was small, they worked well ahead on anthems, and often members took music home to work on as well. So Jill's policy was to let them sing if they were on time for Sunday's warm-up. The commitment to the choir was high among its members, so that worked for them.

Calling absentees let them know they were missed and kept Jill in touch with them. She found as she continued in the position, that it was easier to call someone after they missed one rehearsal than after a month. Keeping in touch with the singers built morale, both Jill's and the singers'. She was also intentional about getting feedback and staying in touch with the feeling level of the choir. She took time to smile, ask the singers how they are, and to listen as they entered and left rehearsal each week. (See also chapter 9.)

Jill set aside a regular time each month for "choir management," the little things that were not directly connected to rehearsals and planning. During this block of time in the summer she sent out recruitment letters to potential members and first rehearsal reminder postcards to members. Throughout the year she followed up on recruitment, and kept on top of short pieces for the church newsletter each month (inviting singers to join the choir, letting the congregation know about special music programs and projects, thanking volunteers, explaining new things the choir is going to do in worship, and listing rehearsal times). She also provided bulletin information (music titles and composers, rehearsal schedules, brief historical notes about new hymns or anthems, announcements about special preludes the congregation might want to come early for, and other upcoming music events).

When the choir did a special program, Jill recruited help from choir members who liked to write short publicity pieces or make posters and programs. Not only did this ease her work load, but the choir members who got involved added energy and new ideas to spark the program.

Management of Other Possible Time-Eaters

There are some other time-eaters that are waiting to tackle church musicians, in addition to those already mentioned. In chapter 1, Jill received an invitation from the president of her denomination's women's group, for the choir to provide music at the district annual meeting. Jill isn't sure about taking on extra singing engagements her first year but the event is right in her own church, and as host church. . . . But what if it opens a floodgate of invitations? Jill makes a note to check with Rev. John about her priorities for the choir to see how he perceives this district event. Then Jill can begin to make an informed decision.

Rev. John sympathizes with Jill's priorities and agrees that if this event was in another church, it would probably be too much at the beginning of her time with the choir. But he knows how important this meeting is to Hope Church's women, so he suggests that Jill consider doing it. He also suggests a simple but elegant anthem to express the day's theme, and reminds Jill that the meeting's theme is the same as the theme for worship two weeks earlier. "Why don't you sing the same piece? It will be familiar to the choir, so no extra rehearsal time for you, and if it's good music (which I know you choose), it will bear repeating."

Gil had a similar problem earlier, in which the men's group wanted him to supply music for their monthly meeting. When he mentioned this to Pastor Lee, she immediately said, "What about Norm? David tells me he's always arriving at bell choir early and sits down to play the piano—hymns, classical pieces, even popular music. He loves to play and definitely plays well enough. I'm sure he would be glad to play for those meetings if he was asked."

Sharon had a similar solution when one of her parishioners caught her after worship one Sunday and asked her to play for his son's birthday party. "I'm sorry, I really don't have the time," Sharon said. "But I have a student who plays very well and could do a good job for you. How long would you like him to play? Were you planning to pay him?"

"Gil, I have this hymn that keeps singing in my head, but I don't know what it is. All I remember is part of the melody line. I think it's in our current hymnal. Please help me find out which hymn it is," begged Sally during the coffee hour after worship.

"Gee, I'll see what I can do," said a confused Gil.

The next morning Gil called his friend, Gloria. "Gloria, I have no idea what to do about this!" He related his conversation with Sally. "I'll know you're a genius if you get me out of this mess, Gloria!"

Gloria laughed. "Start printing up my 'Genius' plaque. It's not as hard as it may seem. I had a choir member come to me once with the second line of a hymn, and I figured it out. One nice thing about hymnals is that they have a metrical index, and that's what you need to use. Count the syllables in the phrases."

"Six and six," replied Gil.

"Okay, now look in the back of your hymnal, at the metrical index. If it's in that hymnal it will be listed under a meter starting with 6.6. Look up those tune names and see which one is your mystery tune.

"Now, when I had the woman with the second-line phrase, I didn't find those words in the hymns with the meter it had. So I went back to our previous hymnal, looked up the meter in the index, checked those tunes, and lo and behold, she was remembering the second line of a final stanza. A friend of mine once had a gospel hymn that was almost impossible to find. He tried the local library's music reference desk and they finally found it."

"You are a true genius, Gloria. Thank you," said Gil.

Chapter Six:
The Substitute Organist or Pianist

"Why didn't someone tell me you sing the 'other' Gloria Patri?"

T hank you so much for meeting me here at church, Sharon," said Laura. "When Gil asked me to play for worship this summer, I really felt overwhelmed. I enjoy playing the piano and occasionally accompanying the choir, but this seems like a lot more. I think I can do it, and I do have the time now that school is over for the summer. I want to do a good job."

"I'm glad you called me," Sharon said with a smile. "I wish I had had someone to call when I first started playing for church. It might have saved me a lot of embarrassing moments! You play well, Laura, that's one reason Gil asked you about the summer. I think I can give you some ideas that will help, and then, after you start the actual playing for worship, you can call me if other questions arise."

Getting Started

"I've brought along a list that I developed the year that I was a substitute organist," Sharon went on. "Going around to different churches I found that I kept having the same questions about playing for worship. Let's look at it together."

1. When is the building open so that I can practice? Is the sanctuary always free to practice in?
2. Where is the switch for the lights that I will need to be able to see the music?

3. Is there an organ or piano key? Where is it kept? Is there a spare key and where is it kept?
4. Where is the "on" switch for the organ? Are there any other switches that need to be turned on as well?
5. Where are the organ speakers or pipes?
6. Does the prelude start before or at the announced time for worship? How long is the prelude generally?
7. Who has to be in the sanctuary or chancel before I end the prelude (pastor, choir, acolyte, and so on)?
8. Are the hymns announced verbally before I play, and how long an introduction is the congregation accustomed to?
9. What service music will I be playing and where is it found? Is it sung as written?
10. When is the offertory prayer: before the offertory, before the Doxology, or after the offertory and Doxology?
11. Do I wait for the ushers to come up the aisle before I play the introduction to the Doxology? Or will they remain standing in the back until I begin? Will I be able to see them?
12. How does the service end, with chimes or a loud postlude?

Laura read quickly through the list, nodding her head. "I think most of my questions are on this list. There are also some things I hadn't thought about."

Sharon began. "You'll be using the organ some, right? It's important to know where the speakers or pipes are. Sometimes the speakers are positioned in the sanctuary in such a way that the organist has a much different perception of the volume than the congregation does. And I am afraid that many complaints center around the loudness or softness of the organ. You can practice hard for weeks on a piece, and the only thing anyone says afterwards is 'Gee, that was loud' or 'It was hard to hear the prelude this morning'! One of the things I want to do with you today before I go is for me to sit at the organ and have you listen, first at the console, then in the choir loft and various places in the sanctuary. That way when you go to play, you'll have a perspective on the volume that the congregation hears, so you'll know when to take their comments seriously and when not to worry.

"Preludes that end on the worship hour can generally be as long or short as you wish, just time them when you practice. If a prelude occurs during the worship (after the announced time for worship) I generally keep it shorter. One church where I substituted had the announcements right on the hour for worship, then I played a short prelude while everyone quietly meditated, then worship began.

"You need to know if someone verbally announces the hymns so you don't start to play while they're speaking—that has embarrassed me when I played in an unfamiliar church. And for introductions, don't 'practice' your hymns right before the congregation sings by always playing the whole hymn through. If the hymn is familiar a short introduction of first and last phrases or just the refrain is usually enough introduction to set the tonality and tempo. If the hymn is new to the congregation it is best to play it all the way through. I usually try to 'solo out' the melody so it is very clear.

"'Soloing out' the melody means playing it on a solo stop, like trumpet or oboe, and playing the left hand on a different manual (keyboard) with softer harmony. Other hymns might seem right if the melody is played alone in octaves, so the congregation can hear it clearly. The organ can be very helpful in these ways to teach a new hymn. One other thing I try to do for new hymns is to find or write a prelude or offertory on the hymn so the congregation can begin to hear the melody in the service before they have to sing it."

"Write a prelude?!" exclaimed Laura. "How am I going to do that?"

"I didn't mean to scare you," laughed Sharon. "I have a large collection of organ music and you are welcome to borrow any of it. Occasionally there will be a new hymn for which no one has written organ or piano music. I've made simple preludes by first soloing out the melody, then putting the melody in the left hand and playing chords in the right hand, then playing the hymn as written to end. It's not as hard as it might sound and it really does help the congregation. You might find that easier to do on the piano at first, if that is where you are most comfortable."

"Okay," said Laura. "What about the question on service music?"

"Well, many churches forget to include a reference number in the bulletin for the service music—the Gloria Patri, the Doxology, and other regularly sung parts of the service. As an organist you need to ask where those pieces are found and if they are sung as written.

Some congregations still sing the Doxology (OLD 100th) in straight quarter notes instead of the half and quarter note combination found in newer hymnals. Sometimes the service music isn't in the current hymnal, as I found when I substituted at one church that used a Kyrie (Lord, have mercy) out of the hymnal from the 1930s. The congregation had been singing it for so long that they didn't need the music, but as a new organist there I certainly did! Coming in new, you might also mention to the church secretary or pastor that it helps other newcomers feel more comfortable if the service music numbers are included in the bulletin."

Hymn Playing

"Are there things I should know about playing the hymns?" asked Laura.

"Well, John Wesley said in his famous instruction to learn them 'exactly as they are printed here' and that's good advice in our time of many new denominational hymnals. Watch for melodies and rhythms that are just a little different from the older books. Watch for rests, and don't be afraid to let go of the keys and REST! Especially on the organ, be rhythmic to help the congregation feel the beat. During your practice mentally or actually sing through all the stanzas so you are aware of any word changes that change the rhythm of the tune. (That practice will also help you avoid playing one too many stanzas on Sunday!) Don't be ashamed to count out hymns that are new to you; learn them correctly from the beginning. Get familiar with the hymns before Sunday so that you can lead the congregation with confidence. That also means that you need to make sure that the pastor or church secretary gives you the hymn numbers in plenty of time for you to practice them."

Preludes, Offertories, and Postludes

"How do I know what to play for preludes and offertories and postludes?"

"The prelude (or opening voluntary as it is often referred to) sets the mood of the worship service so it helps if you know the theme of the service—whether joyous or meditative music is appropriate. The offertory often leads into a doxology, so I like to play an offertory in a related key to the doxology. Postludes (also called closing voluntaries) generally lead people out with energy and joy, but do keep in touch with your pastor because sometimes they like to end reflectively and a quieter postlude would be more effective.

"I use a lot of organ pieces based on the hymns of the service, but generally only one or two of the three pieces will be hymn-based. I try to balance my use of contemporary composers with those from music history. I aim for variety in my pieces not only for the congregation's listening but also for my practicing. I am careful to avoid planning two difficult pieces in one service; it's too stressful. I like to give myself challenges occasionally—to learn new pieces or revive difficult pieces I've done before, but I try to spread that learning out and mix in pieces that I know well or that are easier to play.

"I have two lists that I've made of my organ pieces to help me in my worship planning. The first is coordinated with our denominational hymnal and lists by number in the hymnal the hymn-preludes I have, along with the composer's name and the collection it is in. That is the first list I go to when I get the hymn numbers from the pastor or church office, to find out what pieces I have on the hymns for the day. The second list is a 'key' list, where I have non-hymn pieces listed by the key they are in. Then if I am looking for an offertory to go with a doxology in G major, I can look at the lists for G major or the related keys of C major and D major (and the three related minor keys—G minor, C minor, and D minor). I also use it if I am playing a service in which the opening hymn immediately follows the prelude, or the postlude immediately follows the closing hymn. Then I can coordinate those keys as well."

"How do I know what pieces are 'good enough' to play for church?" asked Laura.

"Well, I like Jane Marshall's 'plastic or sterling silver spoon' theory," replied Sharon. "Plastic spoons do the job of getting food into your mouth, but what you cherish and hand down to your children is your sterling silver. It has a timeless value. That's the kind of music we want to play in worship—music that speaks to the eternalness of God. That's why sometimes I put a note in the bulletin that a Bach piece I am playing has enabled people to worship for over three hundred years. And that's also why I include contemporary sounds in the organ music, for God is speaking still today and in new ways. If the piece has particularly different sounds I do put a note in the bulletin to explain why I am playing it and to guide the congregation's meditation during it."

Getting to Know the Organ

"That's helpful," said Laura. "Now, tell me, what do all these names on the organ stops mean?"

"Another handy list!" said Sharon. "Let's talk about these and listen to them as we begin to play, okay?"

ORGAN TERMS
- The keyboards are called *manuals.*
- The *Swell* is often "under expression" with a volume pedal.
- The *Great* usually contains the loudest stops.
- A third manual is called the *Choir* or *Positiv* and usually contains softer or solo stops.
- On electronic organs *red letter stops* are solo stops (use sparingly with diapasons and flutes 8' and 4' for "bright" hymns); *green letter stops* are string sounds.
- 8' (8-foot) sounds unison pitch.
- 16' (16-foot) sounds one octave lower than unison pitch (note that 16' is the basis for pedal stops).
- 32' (32-foot) sounds two octaves lower than unison pitch (only in the pedal division of very large instruments).
- 4' (4-foot) sounds one octave higher than unison pitch.
- 2' (2-foot) sounds two octaves higher than unison pitch.
- 1' (1-foot) sounds three octaves higher than unison pitch.
- 2 2/3' (2 2/3-foot) sounds a twelfth above unison pitch.
- 1 3/5' (1 3/5-foot) sounds a seventeenth above unison pitch.
- 1 1/3' (1 1/3-foot) sounds a nineteenth above unison pitch.
- Mixtures (2 2/3', 1 3/5', 1 1/3') combine unison, octave, and fifth-sounding pitches (twelfth and nineteenth along with one, two, or three octaves).

SOME COMMON STOPS (IN ALBPHABETICAL ORDER) AND THEIR MEANINGS

Manual Stops	Meaning
clarinet 8'	solo, unison
clarion 4'	trumpet, sounds octave higher
diapason 8'	primary organ tone, unison
dulciana 8'	string, unison
fagott 16'	bassoon, solo, sounds octave below unison
flautino 2'	flute, two octaves above unison
flauto dolce 16'	flute, sounds octave below unison
gedeckt 4'	flute, octave above unison
gedeckt 8'	flute, unison
mixture IV	diapasons, octaves and fifths above unison
nazard 2 2/3'	sounds twelve notes above unison
oboe 8'	solo, unison
octave 4'	primary organ tone, octave above unison
open diapason 8'	primary organ tone, unison
quint 2 2/3'	diapason, twelve notes above unison
rohrflöte 8'	flute, unison
salicet 4'	string, octave above unison
salicional 8'	string, unison
superoctave 2'	diapason, two octaves above unison
trompette 8'	trumpet, solo, unison
trumpet 8'	solo, unison
unda maris 8'	with dulciana, undulating
vibrato	wide undulation
voix céleste 8'	with salicional, undulating

Pedal Stops	Meaning
blockflöte 2'	flute, two octaves above unison
bourdon 8'	flute, unison
diapason 16'	primary organ tone, sounds octave below
mixture IV	diapasons, octaves, and fifths above unison
octave 8'	diapason, unison
posaune 16'	trombone, solo, octave below unison
schalmei 4'	oboe, octave above unison
subbass 16'	flute, sounds octave below
superoctave 4'	diapason, octave above unison
trumpet 8'	solo, unison

Playing the Pedals

"Sharon, what are these marks here around the pedal line of the music: the ^ and ᴗ . I saw them in the method book Gil gave me, too."

"Those are pedal markings, Laura. When we pedal we use both feet, and we use both the heel and toe. The ^ means to use your toe and ᴗ means to use the heel. When the marks are above the staff that indicates your right foot; left foot markings are written below the staff. You notice here on this hymn that there are lots of scale passages for the pedal. That's why I've marked in the pedal so that I can learn the 'footing' (you know, like 'fingering') and always be sure that the line is smooth.

"That reminds me of another 'hymn thing' that beginning organists sometimes do. When you play a hymn, the right hand generally takes the alto and soprano voices, the left hand plays the tenor, and the pedals play the bass line. Some organists play the bass line in both the hands and feet. Give yourself a break, don't double that line.

"I sometimes leave out the pedal for one of the middle stanzas, just for a change, and play all four parts in my hands. Then when the pedal comes back in, I play only the tenor in my left hand.

"The division of parts is one thing that makes 'soloing out' easier. We talked about that earlier. You can take the soprano part on a solo stop in your right hand, the alto and tenor parts in your left hand, and the bass part in the pedals."

Hymn Tempi

"What about tempi for the congregational singing?" asked Laura. "How do I know, other than my memory of singing it before, what a good tempo is?"

"Good question. There are a lot of factors to take into account when deciding the tempo of a hymn: the size of the sanctuary and the length of reverberation in it (that means how long the sound of the keyboard instrument lasts after it is played, like an echo), where the choir is in relationship to the congregation and organ (are they following the organist or are they far away and leading their own tempo), the size and age of the congregation, and the harmonies and phrase lengths of the hymn. Some hymnals now have metronome markings (beats per minute), but that can only be a general guide.

"I find most often that congregational pieces need to go fast enough so that the phrases can be sung in one breath but not so fast that the congregation cannot take a breath in between phrases! Singing it yourself is a good test."

Coda

"I've certainly learned a lot today," said Laura. "Thanks so much, Sharon."

"I'm glad I could help you, Laura. The church needs more good organists. It's not an easy job, but it is a privilege to lead people in worship through music. You know, you probably would enjoy the American Guild of Organists group here in town. We get together once a month during the school year and talk about different organist issues. There are some great folks in the group and it would give you a good perspective on this undertaking. Perhaps the music budget could pay for your membership. Why don't you talk to Gil about it?"

"I will. Thanks again."

Chapter Seven:
Directing a Handbell Choir

"Why do ringers wear gloves?" and other things you need to know

I am really sorry to ask you at such a late date to direct the hand-bell rehearsal, Jill," said David. "But it's an important rehearsal in our preparation for Christmas, so all the ringers need to ring. My wife is going into early labor right now, and I need to be there. My friend, Karen, from Second Church has filled in for me before, and she'd be glad to talk with you, but she can't help Thursday night. Okay? I've got to go."

Jill hung up the phone. Things were certainly never dull at Hope Church. She had never held a bell before, much less directed a hand-bell choir. Well, directing was directing. She could manage. The handbell music was certainly beautiful this time of year, and David made it look easy.

Jill went over to the handbell choir file and picked up the director's folder. Good thing David had left it at church this week. And he was on the ball—notes after last Thursday's rehearsal were on top of the music. He had noted measures to work on for rhythm, one piece that needed the melody brought out, and a section to work on mallet tech-nique. What is "mallet technique"? thought Jill. And what does it have to do with bells? Maybe she had better check with Karen after all.

Getting Started

"Thanks for meeting me here at Second Church, Jill," said Karen. "Our bells are already set up for rehearsal tonight and that makes it easier for me to show you a few things. You haven't ever rung before? Okay. Each ringer is generally responsible for two bells, one for each hand, plus any extra sharps or flats of those two notes.

Notice that the bells are set up like a keyboard, low notes to the left as you stand behind the table, higher notes to the right. Sharps and flats are arranged like the black keys on the piano. Here, put these gloves on. Now, pick up the bell like this. Do you see the clapper? The clapper movement is what makes the bell ring."

After learning to hold one bell and ring it on the beat, Jill added the second bell. She was surprised by the weight of the bells and the preparation and timing needed to ring on the beat.

"Now you're ready to ring a piece," said Karen. "It's a bit different from playing the piano where you read all the notes, or singing where you only read one vocal line. In ringing you need to read your two notes and their accidentals (sharps, flats, and naturals). You are responsible for those two notes. If you don't ring them they will not be heard."

Jill and Karen rang four notes out of a piece for one octave of bells. Even though Jill knew the melody she found herself ringing late because she hadn't thought ahead and prepared to ring on the beat. Watching just one line and one space required a different skill for reading the music, too.

"Enough torture," laughed Karen. "I just wanted you to under-stand what your ringers are going through. Then you can be a better conductor. David's choir has several very good ringers and a few who just started this year with whom you will need to be empathetic. Now you can understand a bit of what they're going through. It will also help your ringers if your beat pattern is very clear and definite when you conduct."

Reading Handbell Music

"Let's look at the music for the rehearsal," continued Karen. At the beginning of each piece there is a chart of bells needed. These three pieces for Christmas all use three octaves of bells. Middle C is called C5; the C below in the bass clef is C4; the C above in the third space of the treble clef is C6. Each C starts a new octave of number-ing; so reading down from middle C (C5) the bells are B4, A4, G4, and so on. When you miss hearing a bell you need to call it by its cor-rect name to alert the ringer who has that bell.

"This marking here 'LV' means 'let vibrate' or don't damp the bell sound by touching the bell to your shoulder. The 'LV' ends here at the ⊕ mark, when all the bells damp at the same time. This second piece has a lot of 'shakes' that look like this in the music: ∿∿∿∿∿ That means that the bells shake rapidly with the clapper striking both sides of the bell.

"The marks in this section that look like *staccato* accents indicate that the higher bells are 'thumb damped.' Thumb damping is one reason we wear gloves—in this technique the thumb is held on the bell and you hear a stopped sound. The *staccato* marks for the lower bells indicate 'plucking.' They are laid on the table pads and the clapper is moved by hand. I don't expect you to remember all this, but you should know that these marks mean something, and ask your ringers if you don't hear a different sound."

"I notice that David's notes say to work on the melody of this third piece. Why is that a problem?" asked Jill.

"Do you remember ringing your two bells? Now, imagine that those two notes occurring within a melody. Each person whose bells are part of the melody needs to ring and damp exactly in synch with the others so that the melody has a flow. If the notes are damped too soon the melody will sound chopped; if they are damped too late the melody will be unclear. In addition to careful damping, the volume of the melody needs to be louder than the accompaniment. See this part here? Sometimes these bells are part of the melody and sometimes they are part of the accompaniment. The ringers not only have to ring on the beat and damp exactly, but they also need to play *forte* (loud) here and *piano* (soft) here. As a director you may need to remind them of these things and listen to see how effective they are in ringing in rehearsal."

"I'm afraid to ask about 'mallet technique,'" said Jill. "It's already a bit more complicated than I expected."

"I think David has done the preliminary introduction to the mallet work on that piece. If I were you, for this one rehearsal, I'd let the experienced ringers in the choir who know how to use the mallets remind the rest. Then let them rehearse using the mallets. They can self-correct for this one rehearsal."

"You've been a big help, Karen. I had no idea there was so much involved in ringing handbells. I certainly will appreciate them more when I listen to them. And I think I have a better sense of what should go on in rehearsal. Thanks."

Other Ideas on Getting Started

Gil looked over the letter from his friend, Ted. He and Ted had grown up together, and now Ted was youth choir director in another state. Ted had written excitedly about the new three-octave set of handbells his church had ordered. "And I get to direct them," the letter went on. "Help me, Gil!"

Dear Ted:
First of all, join The American Guild of English Handbell Ringers, which supplies information to ringers and directors and also holds workshops all over the country. They have a journal with ideas and reviews of new music, and people who can help answer your questions. Until you start getting their information and get to one of their directors' workshops, here are a few tips:

I trust you have the accessories necessary for handbell choirs: tables at a proper height, table pads and covers (we have one set of covers for practice and another for worship, so the worship ones don't get the wear and tear of rehearsals), practice gloves and performance gloves, music stands (or those binders that open to stand), and polish and polishing cloths.

Make sure that people understand the importance of attendance for handbell choir, because it is unlike other choirs. If a ringer is absent, those bells aren't rung or heard, and that can be difficult for other ringers. Whenever someone is going to be absent, it is best to find a substitute ringer. You may find musicians in your church who can't ring on a regular basis who are willing to ring occasionally at rehearsal—but warn them that it's different from playing the piano or singing in choir. Another way to find substitutes in the beginning is from other churches that have rehearsal at a different time.

After your own choir has been going for awhile you will have your own pool of substitutes, people who rang last year who can't commit to every week this year but could come to an occasional rehearsal. It is best if the director is not the substitute ringer, because then the directing doesn't get done, either the actual conducting or the listening to see how the piece is fitting together.

The general way to assign three octaves of handbells is as follows:

If you have more than eleven interested ringers split a position between two of your less secure ringers. Generally it works best to split one of the middle, busier positions, say positions 5 through 7.

Because ringing bells requires intense focus on just two notes (one line and one space), I've found it works better in the beginning to have ringers stay in one position and get comfortable with it. After awhile, some ringers will need to shift around for challenge, but that's down the road for you.

I am enclosing a list and single copies of my favorite beginning handbell pieces. Please return the single copies after you're finished looking at them, because they belong to the music library here at church. It's best to start with pieces in 4/4 or 3/4, with basic quarter, half, dotted half, and whole notes. Avoid pieces with a lot of accidentals this first year, or pieces with more than one key change. In bell ringing, key changes means switching bells, a skill best learned after basic ringing skills are very secure. There are a number of special techniques for bells (thumb damp, pluck, shake, LV, and so on) that should be used only sparingly your first year. My ringers also found it easiest to use music in the beginning that did not have page turns (repeats are okay).

As a beginning director, you will learn a lot if you ring each position (yes, set up the bells and actually ring) for each piece that you direct. The choir will be taking a month to six weeks to learn each piece, so you won't have five pieces to learn at a time. Pick the first two pieces you'd like to play in worship and stand up and ring them. You'll find out which parts are boring, which parts are very busy, and where the tricky spots are.

Notice that bell music has several differences from piano or choral music. First, there is a "bells needed" chart at the top near the title. Those are the only bells that play in that particular piece. Use the assignment chart I gave you, along with your own modifications to assign the bells for each piece. Usually two adjacent positions of the choir will share a folder or three-ring binder to hold the music. Mark the copies with the bell assignments. Later, when your choir is ringing more difficult music you will occasionally also mark bell changes in the music before rehearsals. Always mark in pencil, because as your ringers become more skilled, they will pass you in ringing skills and sometimes will know a better way to do something. (That is hard to take, but is a fact of life for the bell choir director!)

The second difference in bell choir music is that the measures are numbered. This is vital for keeping the choir together and finding a common place in the music. When you rehearse the choir in the beginning it is helpful to have them count aloud, like we used to in beginning band: 1-2-3-4, 2-2-3-4, 3-2-3-4, 4-2-3-4, 5-2-3-4, and so on. After you have practiced each position, mark the more difficult measures in your copy for each ringer so you can watch out for them.

A third difference is primarily for the ease of the middle C (C5) and surrounding ringers. In piano music or a four-part chorale, the notes for the tenor line may range up to F above middle C. In handbell music that note would not be written in the bass clef with ledger lines, but it would move to the treble clef. Middle C and below are always written in the bass clef in handbell music and above middle C is always written in the treble clef. So if you are ringing a hymn, it needs to be written in bell notation, so that the ringers can always find their notes within one clef (and not have their eyes jumping around the page).

In your first rehearsals, concentrate on ringing technique. You want it to look easy but it will take practice to get everyone's arms moving to begin with, then to get their arms moving together and actually ringing the bells. Don't overlook the importance of practicing damping, or stopping the bell sound. Damping technique makes a big difference in the final sound of a piece, whether it is clear, fuzzy, or choppy.

We did a lot of patterns in learning to ring, with left and right hands, such as:

Listen for ringing together on the beat and for clean damping (no "hangover" of notes). Work your first pieces carefully and slowly; don't let sloppy ringing become a habit, even in these beginning days.

It is best to have the bells set up and ready to ring before the rehearsal hour. I've done it two ways: (1) have everyone take turns setting up and cleaning up, or (2) have one group responsible always for setup and one group for cleanup. Although it's nice to rotate the chore, I think it works best when each group has a consistent task, so no one can "forget" it was their turn. Setting up involves getting the tables ready (put on pads and covers), getting the bells out in order, setting up the music and having gloves and sharpened pencils ready. Cleaning up involves wiping the bells with the polishing cloths (it's actually fastest if each ringer wipes his or her own bells), putting the bells in their cases, putting away the music, table covers and pads, and tables. Someday I'm going to have a handbell rehearsal room where the tables, pads, and covers won't have to be put away, and the bell cases won't have to be lugged down two halls and up a stairway to their locked closet. It may only happen in heaven! Oh, well.

We generally have a polishing party at the end of the year (and before Christmas if the bells look dingy). Everyone brings old cloths and one ingredient for ice cream sundaes. Everyone who helps to polish the bells gets to make their own ice cream sundaes when the polishing is done, from the various ingredients everyone has brought.

Because of the work involved in preparing to ring and cleaning up each week, bell choir rehearsals need to be about an hour and a half to be effective. Sometimes that works right before singing choir rehearsal, sometimes not. It is important for everyone to be on time, because it is hard to ring when everyone isn't there yet (there are too many notes missing). If you have to schedule a special room for the bell choir rehearsal be sure to include setup and cleanup times on each end of the rehearsal.

Sunday mornings require special planning for bell choirs. Warm-up time needs to be coordinated not only with worship times in the sanctuary, but also with any other choirs the ringers are involved in. Talk with the other choir directors about the importance of the bell choir's warm-up and negotiate times with them.

When we ring for worship I've found it best to have everyone who possibly can help with both setup and cleanup. Usually the time for setup and warm-up is relatively short, and it is important to refresh the minds and arms by ringing the pieces for worship. After worship people want to see friends and get to dinner, so it is best if cleanup can be done quickly also. In the warm-up time, remind the ringers of any tricky places, then play the piece your best. End the warm-up with the music and bells set for your ringing. Take your gloves with you.

Our choirs most often ring the prelude, so we gather in the

hall outside the sanctuary before service and have a word of prayer together. If we rang during the offertory we would pray at the end of our warm-up. Prayer not only reminds us that we ring to praise God, but it also gives us a time to ask for strengthened arms and focused minds. Your first year you may find that prayer strength especially important!

Whenever you ring during the service, have the ringers process in order to their places at the bell tables, with their gloves on. At your signal they will pick up the bells together, then you will give the preparatory beats. Eye contact really helps in worship, so practice it in rehearsals. If someone gets lost you can give them a measure number so they can enter again. Don't be afraid to say the measure number aloud; the congregation rarely hears it in the midst of the bell sounds.

I know all this sounds like a lot, Ted, but you are in for a lot of fun ahead! Bell choirs not only ring heavenly sounds, but because of the deep time commitment and the special skills learned together, they can also become a tightly knit group. Lead them with love and prayer, and you will all find your-selves growing in music skills, in fellowship, and in praise.

All my best,
Gil

Chapter Eight:
Surviving the Children's Choir Rehearsal

"But they always look so angelic on Sunday!"

Involving Parents for Planning and Support

G race looked around the room, where a good number of parents had shown up for the first children's choir parents' meeting of the year. It was nice to see familiar faces from last year and also some new faces. These were the people whom Grace would count on throughout the year for assistance, support, and commitment. She took a deep breath.

"I want to welcome you all to this first parents' meeting," she said. "Tonight we'll get to know one another a little and talk about the plans for this year's children's choir. Please sign the clipboard that is coming around, with your address, phone, children's names and ages, and what skills you'd like to volunteer. My hope is to involve everyone so that no one has too large a burden. You are the backbone of our children's choir, and I want to thank you for coming tonight and showing your commitment.

"Tonight I want to share the goals I have for the children's choir. If you have other goals you would like us to consider we can talk about those also. I think children's choirs have the wonderful task of providing a place in the church for children to learn in several areas: what the church and faith mean, what worship is about, what it means to work together in a group, and a whole range of musical skills as well. In rehearsals I try to balance learning, fellowship, fun, and performance. All those things can happen when we have an atmosphere of respect for one another and when the expectations are clear.

"The children's choir will sing each month, on the third Sunday at the early service. That is the same as last year, which seemed to work well. Yvonne, could you help pass out these schedules? You will note on the schedules that the third Sunday of December and also the second Sunday of May we will sing at both services. When we sing at the second service, the children have been staying through the children's time in the service, and then leaving quietly. Does that seem okay with everyone?"

"I wonder if we might designate some of the older children to help get the younger ones out better," suggested Marvin. "I hate seeing bewildered children who are not sure where they are supposed to be in worship."

"I think that would work this year," said Grace. "Several of the older children have been in choir for three years now and can be quite responsible. I'll plan to do that." (See also chapter 3 about children and Sunday morning.)

"Can we also designate parents to take turns helping to hang the robes back up? Last year it got to the point where only a faithful few of us were always there. And it can be disaster if the robes are left all over the choir room," said Mary.

"Good idea, Mary. Perhaps those parents who help robe the children that day can make sure the robes get hung back up. Then you would only have to remember one day, instead of one to robe and one to disrobe," suggested Marvin.

"I notice that you have 'caroling and Christmas party' on the schedule," said Harry. "Are you going to the church's shut-ins again, and will you need drivers?"

"Yes to both questions," responded Grace. "That is a good outreach time for the children and the shut-ins really enjoyed it. Your van would be great, Harry."

"Do you want a parent to be at rehearsals this year?" asked Mary. "I enjoyed helping out last year, but I have a class every other week this year."

"What kinds of things did you do?" asked Susan. "I'm new to this, but Katie is finally old enough for choir and she's so excited about singing. I'd kind of like to keep an eye on things so, if it's not too difficult, perhaps I could help the weeks you can't, Mary."

"Having an assistant in rehearsals is a big help to me," said Grace. "Mary did things like taking attendance, helping to pass out music and instruments, helping to manage the children when we went up to the sanctuary for practice, and helping with cleanup after rehearsal. Having another adult around also helps with managing behavior problems."

"I'd rather make phone calls again this year, if that's okay," volunteered Harry. "I'll call when any child misses twice in a row to check on them, and anyone who misses the rehearsal before a performance. Do you have some prospective singers for me to call this year too?"

"Did you meet the new family last week in church?" asked Marvin. "What was their name . . . Hamptons, Harrington?"

"Oh, yes. The church office gave me their names, the Harmons. They have two children the right age for our choirs," said Grace. "They've just moved into the neighborhood, and seem interested in getting involved. I can find their number for you, Harry."

"Will you make up a robing/disrobing schedule for parents, Grace? And will you be needing help with the Christmas program? Do you want me to help again in worship, getting the children in their spots for singing?"

"Yes, yes, and yes, Yvonne," laughed Grace. "The Christmas program will be done in conjunction with the Sunday school so teachers and some parents will be helping from that area as well. That way more children will be involved, but more adults too. I've been talking with Linda, our Sunday school superintendent, and she has some good ideas. If several of you would like to get involved with the Christmas program I would be glad to have you attend the next planning meeting with me on Saturday morning at 10:00 at Linda's house. Her address is in the church directory."

"My big question is 'Are we staying with the Sunday rehearsal time?'" spoke up Tom. "I really liked not having to plan an extra weekday last year, especially with my boys' sports schedules."

"That appears to be the general consensus," said Grace, as she looked around and saw nodding heads. "Do we need to plan any refreshments for the children?"

"Goodness, no. My children eat too many cookies in Sunday school as it is," exclaimed Mary.

Tapes, Word Sheets, and Copyright Issues

"Will the children be bringing home tapes or word sheets to help them learn the anthems? Katie's school does that and it helps the children learn the music between rehearsals," asked Susan.

"That's one thing I wanted to ask this group," replied Grace. "Do you find that helpful? It does cost us to reprint words or make tapes of copyrighted pieces, but if the cost is worth it, we'll do it."

"Let's do stay clean around copyright," said Harry. "One of the teachers' workshops I attended this summer was really stressing the limits of our use of copyright materials, and paying our fair share for use. I certainly hope the church is setting a good example in this area."

"I agree, Harry," said Grace. "That's why I wanted to make sure the tapes are helpful, because if you want them we will need to clear permission to copy the songs and pay the fees. This year we will be using both new and old pieces from the hymnal too. Some of the older hymns are in the public domain, and so copyright is no longer a problem."

"You know, I really like using the tapes. We make it part of the nighttime routine at our house," said Mary. "It is helpful to have the word sheets, too. Sometimes my children come home with strange 'words' to the anthems and if I can't tell from the tape, we're out of luck."

"I see other nods too," said Grace. "So we'll plan to send home tapes and word sheets at the first rehearsal. Yes, Harry, we will get word copyright permission, too. That about covers what I had on my agenda for this meeting. I'm looking forward to a good children's choir year here at Hope Church. Shall we adjourn to Marvin's special cookies?"

Planning for the Children's Choir

Gil sat down at his desk to consider the children's choir for the coming year. It was good to have some things in order this fall at Second Church. Since he had started late last spring, he now had a better idea of who the children were, who were strong singers, and who needed some support. Gil had picked up a good idea at his summer workshop to try: Placing the stronger singers in a group behind the weaker singers. Before he had always paired strong and weak singers, but that seemed to make the strong singers weaker. This other way should have the advantage of strengthening the strong singers and still supporting the weaker singers.

The rehearsal space should work well this year, too. The children's choir had moved to one of the Sunday school rooms. The chairs were child-size, the tables were the right size for working or for playing instruments, and there was a rug to sit on for informal times. The room was well ventilated with adequate lighting, coat hooks, and a closet for the instruments nearby. The piano had been tuned for fall. Gil had worked carefully with the Christian education committee and the teacher of this particular classroom to ensure cooperation. He was always careful that the room was left after rehearsal as he had found it.

Instruments and Children

While he was thinking about it, Gil walked down the hall to the instrument closet. It was probably a good idea to see that the instruments were in good shape and dust-free. He felt fortunate that several years ago Second Church had invested in a set of Orff instruments: xylophones, metallophones, glockenspiels, and rhythm instruments. The barred instruments helped turn hymns into anthems. Repeated patterns could be played by most of the children on the instruments and helped them with rhythm skills, as well as the skill of playing the instrument. And the instruments were a good treat for well-behaved children.

Gil checked that all the bars on the glockenspiels, metallophones, and xylophones were accounted for, along with the extra sharps and flats that were used occasionally. It was great to be able to remove the unused bars to simplify playing by the youngest children, but it was easy to mix up the unused bars from the different instruments. Gil also counted the mallets and made sure that there were enough pairs for each instrument, as well as spares.

The rhythm instruments were often treated less carefully than the barred instruments. Gil untangled triangles and their holders and beaters, sand blocks (which needed fresh sandpaper), wood blocks (one with a loose handle to repair), finger cymbals, hand cymbals, maracas, hand drums of various sizes, castanets, a snare drum, bongos, and umpteen rhythm sticks. He checked for smooth edges, not wanting to have to do any splinter removal during rehearsals, and sturdy handles. After repairing the sand blocks and wood blocks, he made a note to order four more pairs of rhythm sticks. It was nice to have enough rhythm sticks for each child when they were working on learning new rhythms.

Music for the Children's Choir

Gil had planned a tentative schedule for the children's choir when he scheduled the adults. Then he had given the list of proposed anthems to Carol, who served as the children's choir librarian. Carol had checked on the number of whole copies of the anthems that he wanted (yes, the children's choir occasionally turned in two halves of anthems). She had given him a list of how many copies there were of each anthem, so Gil could figure out how many additional copies to buy for this year's choir (plus a few extras), along with the other pieces that would be new to the choir library. Carol was a big help in keeping track of the children's music, getting it in and then out of their folders, and helping to get the copyright permissions from various publishers for the word sheets they sent home with singers.

Gil looked over the list of children's choir anthems again. Yes, he did have a good balance—easy and challenging, one piece to stretch their range, one piece that focused on the instruments, and a good balance of hymn anthems and free compositions. One of Gil's convictions was that the children's choir was a training choir for children to learn to worship for the rest of their lives. To that end, he liked to include hymns, not only the ones that would be sung the Sundays the choir sang in worship, but also hymns as anthems. The more the children know the music of the church, the hymns and service music, the more comfortable they will be as teenagers and adults in worship, Gil reasoned.

Other Details

Now to the housekeeping work for the choir. First, Gil checked that registration forms were available. These included pertinent and useful information such as a child's name, address, phone, age, grade, birthday, parent(s)' names, whether or not the child attends Sunday school, any musical instruments played, height for robing, and folder number. Gil then checked the schedules with all rehearsals and performance times, the folder list and robe list for him and Carol, schedules for parents to help with robing and treats, the proposed anthem list with dates and titles and composers for the church office, a schedule of rehearsals and other activities for the church office, birthday postcards and stamps (to be sent out throughout the year), "we missed you" postcards for absentees, and a covenant for choristers.

The covenant helped children understand the importance of commitment to the choir (attendance and attention) and contained some simple rules along with places for Gil and the child to sign. At the first rehearsal he talked with the children about God's covenants in the Bible—the rainbow, the Ten Commandments, and Jesus, the new covenant. After Gil explained that he and the children each had a part in the covenant, to work together, everyone signed the covenant and each child received a copy.

Earlier in the summer, recruitment letters had gone out to the parents, with postcards to each child in the age range of the choir. Now it was time to publicize the pizza party that helped to kick off the Wednesday after-school program at church, which included the children's choir. Gil had planned the party with the Christian education committee, which was responsible for the Wednesday program. Although he was trying to keep his meetings to a minimum, he found that going to the yearly planning meeting of this committee really helped him stay in communication with the Sunday school teachers and those who carried out the extra children's programs in the church.

At the yearly planning meeting they coordinated dates and programs, and negotiated times. Gil really appreciated this planning time and the fact that the Christian education and music programs honored the time commitments of the other. In his last church he felt stepped on several times when Christian education would schedule something on a Sunday morning when the children were singing or at a rehearsal time. By working with the Christian education committee at Second Church, Gil kept communication lines open and could remind them that choir is also a part of children's Christian education.

The pizza party provided a good time of fellowship, got children there who might not have showed up at an ordinary first rehearsal, and gave Gil a chance to know the children a little better. He tried to include at least one other social event during the year, generally letting the choir parents help to decide what the event would be and letting them do the planning and production of the event. Then he was freer to be with the children. Including these times of fun and fellowship seemed to help his relationship with the children, making them more willing to concentrate and respect his control in rehearsals. Gil had found that providing an orderly and loving atmosphere in rehearsals got the results he wanted in cooperation and attentiveness.

It all looks in order, Gil thought. I've missed the children over the summer; it will be good to start up rehearsals again and learn and sing together.

Chapter Nine: Personal Relationships and Avoiding Burnout

"Why do I only hear the complaints?"

Working with the Congregation

L aura practiced hard for her first Sundays at the organ. Within the first month, she had heard two complaints about her playing in worship—one about the loudness of the organ (overheard during the coffee hour following worship) and one that the hymns were too fast (from her elderly neighbor, who attended the same church). She also received one compliment (from the pulpit—thank you, Pastor Lee), thanking Laura for filling in.

The children's choir was doing very well this year, Gil thought. The first time they sang, things were a little ragged, but by the second time everything went very smoothly. The third time the children sang, a note appeared in Gil's box. "The children are TOO NOISY in worship. Why can't they have Sunday school during that time? Worship is for adults!"

Laura's feelings were hurt by the overheard comment the most. Since she was not told directly, she felt (and perhaps rightly so) that it wasn't a serious complaint. Still, Laura double-checked the volume question with her friend Karen, who was sitting in the congregation, and Karen reassured her that the organ was not too loud.

The overheard remark still bothered Laura. If she was going to continue to play for worship at Second Church she would have to find a way to let people know that if they had a legitimate concern about her playing, she couldn't fix it unless someone talked to her. She did have the best interests of the church and its worship at heart.

What Laura wanted was to build a relationship with the congregation so that people could feel free to bring her praise and concern. She had found that being at the keyboard for the prelude before many people came to worship, and being there again while people left after worship limited the number of people she had contact with before and after worship. So Laura decided to be sure to attend the coffee hour after worship (even when she felt worn out or disappointed about her playing after service) and also to keep in touch with people through the other social events of the church. That way her natural friendliness and concern would be seen by the congregation. It turned out that these were good decisions because over the year even if Laura was occasionally disappointed about her playing, someone inevitably came up to say how much they enjoyed it. (She found out when she mentioned this to Pastor Lee that this often happened to pastors about the sermon, too!)

When Laura's neighbor first mentioned the tempo of the hymns, Laura was taken aback and didn't know what to say. Her neighbor, realizing that Laura was bothered by her remark, quickly jumped into the void. "I'm sure it's just because you're new at this, but some of us just can't sing that fast anymore."

Laura regained her composure. "Which hymn was too fast?" she asked cautiously. "Or is it just in general that the hymns don't feel comfortable?"

"Well, that new one. You know, I've never sung it before and trying to figure out the tune and read those words, I just felt left behind. I guess the other ones were okay, because I knew them."

"That makes sense to me. Perhaps on a newer hymn I need to give the congregation a little more time to coordinate music and words. I've learned the hymn by practicing it, usually for several weeks, and I forget that you are seeing it for the first time."

"That sounds good, honey. I didn't mean to hurt your feelings, because I am proud to see you playing, but I love the hymns and it bothers me to feel like I cannot sing them."

Gil looked up from reading the anonymous note in his box. Pastor

Lee was standing nearby, and she asked, "Is anything wrong, Gil? You look concerned."

Gil showed her the note.

"I'm sorry about this," she said. "There is a group in the church who would be glad for all children to be banished to Sunday school, never to return. You know from working with the Christian education committee how they have to fight that attitude sometimes. The kids are doing great, and I think they are a wonderful addition to our worship when they sing. I never pay attention to anonymous notes, at least that's my principle. It's true some of them haunt me in the middle of the night. But if someone really felt they had a legitimate concern they would have the conviction to sign their name or talk to you in person. Or at least, I think we've tried to make it clear that the congregation has access to the staff-parish committee members if they feel they have a complaint and can't come to one of the staff."

"I guess you're right, but criticisms still sting," said Gil. "Especially when they're about 'my children.' The children are working hard this year and I feel like we have a great rapport. Do you think this note reflects very many people's feelings?"

"No, Gil, I don't. I think that only four or five people out of our whole congregation of five hundred hold that opinion. I hope those numbers can help put this in perspective for you," answered Pastor Lee.

"Yes, that does help," admitted Gil. "So, what other words of wisdom are you going to impart at our staff meeting?"

"Better come and see," replied Pastor Lee with a laugh.

Working with Choir Members and Parents of Children's Choir Members

Jill had sung in the choir the year before she was asked to direct, and she knew that certain singers liked to do solos. After she became director she talked to those persons when she was planning the year's schedule and asked them about singing solos for worship. She had thought that by taking the initiative and scheduling them for solos she could avoid complaining or miffed singers.

But as Christmastime approached Jill noticed one of the sopranos giving her the cold shoulder. After twice dropping friendly remarks that were ignored, Jill decided to take the initiative again. After rehearsal she stopped Millie and asked her if anything was wrong.

"Of course not," snapped Millie. "Although, I can't believe you are going to let June sing that solo on Christmas Eve. She'll positively embarrass the choir."

Jill blinked. Of course, she remembered, Millie had always done the solo on Christmas Eve. She really hadn't thought about it being so special. Millie had sung the Thanksgiving solo this year and Jill was trying to spread the solo work among various singers. June had a lovely voice but hadn't done much solo work. Jill had been coaching her and had had her try the solo in choir once.

Jill thought fast. "Well, I think June will do okay. I've been working with her and she's made a lot of progress this fall. Your Thanksgiving solo was so wonderful; have you thought about what solo you'd like to sing during Lent or Eastertime?"

"Now that you mention it, I had thought of singing something from *Messiah* this spring. Could you help me go over several choices after choir next week?" Millie asked.

"That would be great, Millie," replied Jill with a silent sigh of relief.

Grace had set a goal for herself this year to stay in good communication with the choir parents. She hated hearing after the fact that so-and-so was upset about choir and was quitting. Grace and Jill had talked over the summer and decided that a little "maintenance" work might go a long way toward keeping everyone happy.

Grace made a point to have the rehearsal room ready with an assistant there to help guide the children in music activities after Grace greeted them. Then Grace could greet the child's parent and ask how things were going, mention a particularly good thing that involved their child in rehearsal lately, or ask about a behavior that seemed different recently.

The choir parents' meeting had opened channels of communication and this weekly maintenance, in addition to following up on absences to let parents know their children were missed, seemed to be working. Grace also took care to thank parents whenever they did anything to help the choir, however small, not only privately but also publicly when possible.

Getting Helpful Feedback

"That sounds great," Gil said to his choir. "Now, tonight before we end rehearsal—yes, we still have ten more minutes—I would like your help. Laura, would you pass out these papers. Thank you.

"I've been directing you for about six months now and I would like some feedback from you. You know I'm very proud of all of your hard work. Last Sunday's anthem was particularly well sung.

"Each week at rehearsal I give you feedback on your singing, and now I'd like some feedback from you. This can help me grow and be more responsive to you. It won't take long. First, please write down something you enjoy about choir—what keeps you coming every week. Second, please write two things that I do that are helpful and that you like. Third, please write two things that you wish I would change. If you can only find one thing or none at all, that's okay, too." (Laughs from the choir.)

"You don't need to sign this, just put it on the piano when you're done. I can't promise I'll change everything at once, but I do want to hear your concerns. Thanks for a good rehearsal."

Gil sat at his desk and made some notes for next week's rehearsal while the choir jotted down their feedback. He looked forward to reading their thoughts. When Gil had asked his friend Gloria about getting helpful feedback she had suggested this. She did it about every year and a half at her church, and found it to be a good indicator of how the choir perceived their working together.

Gathering positive feedback in the first two items helps to avoid getting overwhelmed with negative criticism, but still gives people room to write things that bother them. Reading the comments at home will give Gil some distance and objectivity, and time to think about how he wants to deal with the criticisms. Ask for this kind of feedback when you and the choir are on an even keel, not at a time of negativity, so that the feedback will have some objectivity.

Gil will check out any bothersome comments with a trusted person on the church staff or someone else who knows his work. For the most part, Gil found that he got a warm feeling from the positive remarks that more than balanced out the challenges for his work.

"David, this is Roy from church calling. How are you?"

"Fine, I just got in from the handbell choir rehearsal at church. How are you?"

"Great. I'm calling you because of my position at church on the staff-parish committee. We just finished our meeting, and we decided to try something new this year to both funnel feedback to each of you and hopefully to facilitate your work together. Each of us on the committee is going to be a liaison for a staff person. I picked you because I think you're doing great, and I won't have to deal with any problems this year!"

"I hope that's true," laughed David. "What exactly does this liaison mean?"

"I'm your link to the staff-parish committee. If you have any concerns about your relationships with other staff or the congregation, I'm here to listen and help, and to take those concerns to the committee for you. If you ever need to meet with us, I'm there to be your support. And for the next two Sundays, and in the newsletter too I think, they are going to list our names together to let the congregation know that if they have any concerns and feel they can't go directly to you, that they can come to me."

"That sounds good to me. You know before Rev. John came, the staff used to be reviewed once a year with the committee. It was really frightening. We would go in and hear all the criticisms everyone had saved up for a year. It was very painful and not very productive. I'm glad we're taking a different way now. By the way, how did the church softball team do last night?"

Working with Church Staff

Pastor Lee's thanks to Laura from the pulpit on Sunday morning (at the beginning of this chapter) gave her a big boost, making her hard work seem worth it. Laura remembered how good it felt being in the choir when they had been praised by the liturgist or pastor after they had sung or when phrases from the anthem found their way into prayers or sermons that day. Now that she was on the staff of the church it made her look at things differently. She wondered about the criticisms and praise that Pastor Lee heard. When was the last time Laura had told Pastor Lee that something she had done was helpful? Maybe it was also time to ease out of the gossip sessions that occasionally popped up in church groups. It didn't seem right to publicly criticize the people she was working with. Laura wondered if Pastor Lee ever wished people would talk with her directly like Laura had wished. This working at church definitely made Laura think differently about some of the things that went on there.

Jill's choir shaped up the processional for Palm Sunday and Easter. On Easter things looked good and the choir sang the introit beautifully. When the second hymn was announced, the one with the soprano descant on the final stanza, the liturgist announced that only the first verse would be sung, in the interest of time. The sopranos looked at Jill dismayed—all that hard work for nothing!

Jill swallowed her frustration. The bulletin even listed the descant on the last stanza. Hymn stanzas are so short, it wouldn't have taken more than probably two extra minutes to sing the whole hymn! Why couldn't the sermon be shortened or one of the prayers, or surely the announcements? Well, she would make an appointment with Rev. John later next week to find out why that decision was made, and to let him know she was disappointed for the sopranos.

How Jill approaches the pastor can make a big difference in the outcome of their discussion. If she goes in angry and then dredges up any other criticisms she has, there is sure to be trouble. Jill has already shown wisdom in not tackling the pastor or liturgist immediately after worship and demanding justice. What she does do after worship is to empathize with the sopranos and suggest other times when they might use the descant—another Sunday of Easter, or at the spring concert.

Jill has heard horror stories of pastors who would not listen to musicians, pastors who were "always right." She feels fortunate that Rev. John has tried to treat her as a teammate and to honor her gifts. That's why this cut in worship hurts. Liturgists at Hope Church stuck closely to the printed page, so Jill didn't think they would have made such a decision. If Rev. John made the decision, why couldn't he tell her before the service, since he obviously had to tell the liturgist then, for they sat on opposite sides of the chancel? It probably doesn't help to keep worrying about it, Jill decides, and makes the appointment for Tuesday with the hope of convincing Rev. John to schedule the hymn for another Sunday of Easter so the sopranos can do the descant.

Before the appointment Jill lists on paper the problem as she sees it, trying to be objective. She also lists the good things Rev. John has done for her and the choir, to put it all in perspective. Then she lists her solution (singing the hymn another Sunday) and what she hopes will come out of their discussion—better communication. Last, but certainly not least, Jill prays for Rev. John, for their relationship and for Hope Church.

"We're not here right now but we want to talk with you. Please leave a message after the beep."

"Roy, this is David calling. I just wanted to let you know about a situation that developed at church. I think it's worked out now, but I wanted to keep you on board. The handbell choir is playing in a festival next Saturday and it's been on the church calendar for about six months. Yesterday when I walked into church I saw signs up all over publicizing a youth barbecue on Saturday at the same time as the festival. You know that about half the bell choir are youth involved in the youth group. I asked in the church office who was planning the barbecue and found out that the program director had decided the previous day that the weather was going to be great on Saturday and it would be a good time to get the kids together. The program director was in her office so I went and explained to her about the handbell festival and the youth who would be torn between these two groups' commitments. After a moment she realized that she had not looked at the church calendar before planning the event, and she decided to move it to the following week. I think we parted friends. Just wanted to keep you on board. Thanks."

"Beep!!!!"

"Gil, do you have a moment? I really need the information for Sunday's bulletin as soon as possible. It's Friday and I don't work tomorrow."

"Oh, Sarah. I'm so sorry. I meant to leave that information for you last Sunday. Here, let me dig it out of my desk. Okay, the anthem title is. . . ."

"Hi, Sylvester. How are you today?" smiled Jill.

"I'm doing okay. The Lord is taking good care of me," Sylvester smiled back.

"That's good to hear. And thank you for polishing my desk last week; it looks great. You certainly do a good job keeping our church in order."

"You know I'm glad to polish that desk anytime you get it clear," laughed Sylvester. "It sure does seem to get piled with papers and music. Do you want the chairs set up differently for rehearsal this week? I noticed the room was rearranged after rehearsal last week."

"No, the usual setup, please. We just ended rehearsal by singing in quartets instead of sections, so we moved the chairs around."

"We do that at my church some, too. Gloria's got a new piece for us that is just wonderful. Would you like to hear it?"

Taking Care of You

"There are plenty of things to keep a church musician busy, learning new music, planning for rehearsals and Sundays, maintaining relationships with singers and ringers and congregations and staff, and managing the myriad of details that choir programs entail. Where do you get fed? Let's use that as our luncheon table discussion topic today," said the president of the local church musicians' fellowship.

"That's a tough question for me this year," said Jill. "It's my first year doing all these things and I feel overwhelmed more than I would like. How do you all do it?"

"I give myself fifteen minutes a day to play pieces I like," said Sharon. "That way I don't mind so much all the other things I have to practice. That's my meditation time."

"I ride my exercise bike—no, don't groan!" said David. "After a grueling rehearsal, I go home and ride furiously (after a warm-up, of course). For the first ten minutes I don't let myself think about everything I have to do, or how the rehearsal went. By the end of the first ten minutes sometimes I'm ready to plan my work, and other times I just enjoy moving my own body. I'm not a health nut, but I know I think and feel better when I take that time."

Gil spoke next. "I have a friend I grew up with, Ted, who works in a church in another state. I can call him and discuss our lives and our church work. That support keeps me going. Sometimes, when I can't afford to call, I think about our friendship and pray for him and his work. I know he's doing the same for me, and that helps."

"I really find my family supportive of my church work. It makes a big difference for me to be able to share my concerns about the church at home. Sometimes it's talking with my husband, sometimes it's just reading a story with my daughters, that puts me back into perspective," said Grace.

"I'm more like David," said Karen. "I like to take walks and take time to think while I'm moving."

"It's the summer workshops I go to that feed me," said Gloria. "Being there with other church musicians from all over reminds me about the importance of the work we do. I get great ideas there and have friends now from lots of different places, all with the same kinds of struggles about church music that I have. And the worship experience there has never failed to help me really *worship*—something I don't always feel I get to do on Sunday mornings, rushing around and being involved with all the details."

Laura said, "I'm just beginning, like Jill, but I feel that I am spending time every day now on work for church. Since I've been playing for church, I've found it really important to have my devotional time each morning. It keeps my faith strong and in tune, and that's what I need each day."

"You know," said Jill, "I think I've found what will nurture me: being at meetings like this and finding friends like all of you to share with!"

Asking for Help Before It's Too Late

At the close of the luncheon, the president of the church musicians' fellowship spoke again. "It looks like you have had some good discussion to go along with the good food. The executive committee has been concerned about the amount of burnout we've seen among church musicians in the last ten years. Many of the people who were working when some of us started are no longer in church music, because they just wore out.

"We on the executive committee want to let you know that we value your work and we value you. We're here to support you, but you need to know yourself, to know when you need to ask for help. Please ask before you burn out, and end up leaving church music.

"Schedule your time. Learn to say 'no' nicely, and without guilt. Get choir members involved in the work that they could do for you and the choir. Ask for support from your pastor, the church office staff, from the parents of your children's choir members. Ask before you get desperate, then your request will sound better! Get to know these other musicians here, because we all have ideas to share, and things we've tried that have and have not worked.

"Give yourself time to talk with God. Remember why you got involved in church music to begin with. Listen to a good piece of church music and let it feed your soul. Remember the good times you have had with your choirs, playing the organ in worship, working with children or handbell ringers.

"It's okay not to be 'super director.' God loves each of us the way we are. And it is God's work that we want to do in our work. Let your faith and God's love support you in your task.

"Now I think our vice-president has an announcement about next month's meeting."

CODA: The Rewards

("There are quite a few!")

Well, Jill and Gil and their companions have gotten off to quite a start together in their first year in their respective churches. You have seen the challenges they have faced and some possible solutions.

One of the rewards for a choir director was hinted at when Gil asked for the written feedback from his choir. It is wonderful to hear why people come to choir and know that part of the reason is because you make them glad to be there. It is a privilege to lead persons in discovering the bonds between music and the Spirit. It is a joy to watch people who dragged their bodies into a rehearsal after a grueling day, leave revived and smiling again. It can touch your heart to find that music has pulled someone through a crisis of which you had not an inkling. You can find the great joy that comes when persons under your leadership discover and develop their musical gifts for the good of God. You can feel the touch of the Spirit when everything comes together in worship and you know God has been present in the music.

One of my greatest joys has been working with children. Young minds are open and growing, and you have been given a privilege to help shape those minds for God and the church. Your own mind will be given new insights and challenges by the questions these children ask you as you consider faith issues together. You can see their eyes sparkle when you all know that the anthem was well done. And there is nothing like the love that children give back to a director who loves them.

Gil's letter to his friend Ted spelled out some of the special pleasures of handbell directing—heavenly sounds from the bells, the camaraderie of closely working together, the trust that develops from having to depend on one another to be there and to ring at the right time! Handbell choirs consider pieces well performed as a special blessing, because it takes so much concentration and teamwork.

Albert Schweitzer once wrote a letter to a friend, saying what a privilege it is each Sunday morning to sit at the instrument that so many great composers sat at and wrote for, to lead a group of people in lifting their voices to the God who made the universe. Surely playing for worship is more than just turning pages and getting all the notes right (or wrong).

Your own growth in musical skills can go hand in hand with your spiritual growth, and your learning to work with all kinds of people. You will make friendships not only in your own church, but also in the larger church around the globe—wherever human beings seek to worship the One who made us and sustains us.

As Jill found at the church musicians' fellowship, there are a lot of really nice people in this church music field. You are now one of them. We can help encourage one another, share ideas and struggles, and find ourselves strengthened as musicians and as Christians along the way. So don't be afraid to reach out, ask a question, find an answer. It is your openness and willingness to work with others that will enable your work to be effective.